# WALKING
# THE SHROPSHIRE WAY

## About the Author

John Gillham was born in Bournemouth, Dorset but now lives with his wife Nicola in Hoddlesden, a small village in the West Pennine Moors.

John has been a full-time professional writer, illustrator and photographer since 1989. His first book, *Snowdonia to the Gower: A Coast to Coast Walk Across Highest Wales*, has been described as one of the classic books on Wales. He also pioneered three other long-distance routes: Lakeland to Lindisfarne, Pennine Ways (an alternative Pennine Way) and the Bowland–Dales Traverse, all of which were published in book form. John's recent books include *The Pictorial Guides to the Mountains of Snowdonia Volumes 1–4*, *Best Day Walks in Snowdonia*, the AA's *Leisure Guide Wales*, and Cicerone's *The Cumbria Way* and *Hillwalking in Shropshire*.

John writes regularly for *The Great Outdoors* (TGO) and has written occasionally for *Dalesman*, *Cumbria Magazine* and *Lakeland Walker*. He has written and contributed to many AA publications. He has twice won Outdoor Writers & Photographers Guild Award for Excellence, firstly for his guidebook *Best Day Walks in Snowdonia* and secondly for the outdoor book *Coast-to-Coasting* (with Ronald Turnbull).

### Other Cicerone guides by the author
*Hillwalking in Shropshire*
*The Cumbria Way*

# WALKING
# THE SHROPSHIRE WAY

## A TWO-WEEK CIRCULAR TRAIL INCLUDING THE WREKIN, STIPERSTONES AND WENLOCK EDGE

### by John Gillham

JUNIPER HOUSE, MURLEY MOSS,
OXENHOLME ROAD, KENDAL, CUMBRIA LA9 7RL
www.cicerone.co.uk

© John Gillham 2019
First edition 2019
ISBN: 978 1 78631 008 8

Printed by KHL Printing, Singapore
A catalogue record for this book is available from the British Library.
All photographs are by the author unless otherwise stated.

© Crown copyright 2019 OS PU100012932

### Updates to this guide

While every effort is made by our authors to ensure the accuracy of guidebooks as they go to print, changes can occur during the lifetime of an edition. Any updates that we know of for this guide will be on the Cicerone website (www.cicerone.co.uk/1008/updates), so please check before planning your trip. We also advise that you check information about such things as transport, accommodation and shops locally. Even rights of way can be altered over time. We are always grateful for information about any discrepancies between a guidebook and the facts on the ground, sent by email to updates@cicerone.co.uk or by post to Cicerone, Juniper House, Murley Moss, Oxenholme Road, Kendal, LA9 7RL.

Register your book: To sign up to receive free updates, special offers and GPX files where available, register your book at www.cicerone.co.uk.

*Front cover:* Passing the Devil's Chair on the Stiperstones ridge

# CONTENTS

## Acknowledgements

I would like to thank my wife Nicola for being a lovely companion on the hills and for proofreading the book before publication; my good friend Ronald for sharing his knowledge of Shropshire's geology; the wonderful hospitality shown to us by the good people of the county, including campsite wardens, innkeepers and the many cheerful bus drivers who took us to some of the remote corners. Many thanks must go to the Shropshire Way Association including their chairman, Audrey Menhinick, with whom I have been collaborating and sharing information from the start, and the route champions' co-ordinators Gill Pursey and Trevor Allison and their teams, who have worked so hard to make sure the routes are all way-marked and free from obstructions. They've also proofread my text and suggested the necessary changes. Last but not least, Helen Beresford with Shropshire Council Outdoor Partnerships Team and their volunteers, who have helped resolve route anomalies.

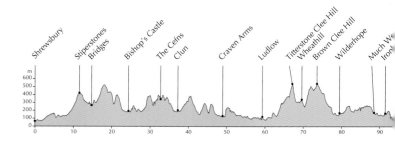

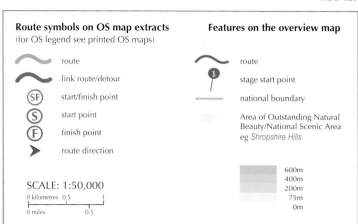

**Route symbols on OS map extracts**
(for OS legend see printed OS maps)

~ route

~ link route/detour

(SF) start/finish point

(S) start point

(F) finish point

➤ route direction

SCALE: 1:50,000

0 kilometres  0.5  1

0 miles  0.5

**Features on the overview map**

~ route

① stage start point

— national boundary

Area of Outstanding Natural Beauty/National Scenic Area
eg *Shropshire Hills*

600m
400m
200m
75m
0m

**GPX files** for all routes can be downloaded free at www.cicerone.co.uk/1008/GPX.

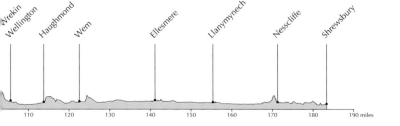

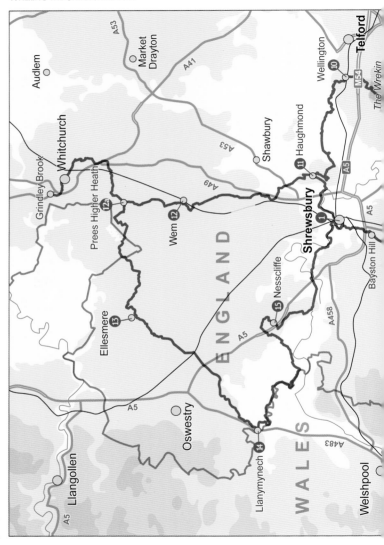

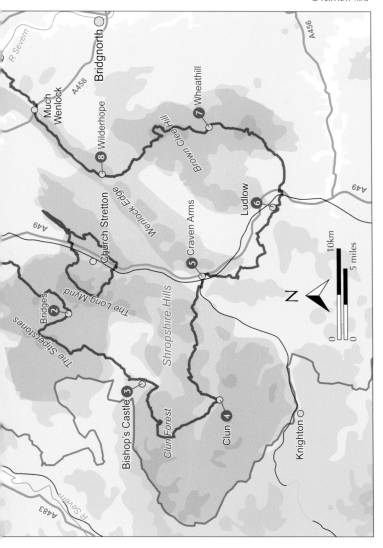

9

*Manstone Rock from Cranberry Rocks, Stiperstones*

# FOREWORD

*Descending Small Batch with Ragleth Hill ahead*

Although devised as a long-distance path, by 2014 the original Shropshire Way had become obscured in a network of routes throughout the county. In 2016, in order to recover the original route, I re-constituted the Shropshire Way Association. Our aim was not only to restore but also to preserve the Shropshire Way for the future. The decision was taken to build a website to act as a guide to walkers with the possibility of a guide-book at a later date.

I encountered the Shropshire Way in 1983 when I bought the first guide by Robert Kirk. Beginning with circular walks based on the route, I walked my first complete circuit in 2008 when the distinctive black and white buzzard waymarks were still in place. This was replaced by a re-designed waymark when Shropshire Council decided to introduce many alternative routes to the long-distance path.

The Association has negotiated and worked with Shropshire Council to identify a main route, design a new waymark and improve the footpath. I am proud and delighted that 10 years on we have launched Shropshire Way Main Route with distinctive orange, black and white waymarks.

I was delighted when John Gillham contacted me early in 2018 to say that Cicerone Press needed a guidebook to simplify the plethora of routes. John was the ideal person to write the guide being already familiar with the Shropshire Hills and very experienced in writing walking guides. Since then we have been working in partnership to retain the stages of the route, already established by the Association and to keep the data consistent across both media. John's excellent route directions ideally complement the website which aims to make the route clear without including detailed directions.

This guide is an invaluable companion to anyone wishing to complete the whole circuit of around 200 miles or for those who wish to make several visits to Shropshire completing a few stages at a time. You will find supplementary information on places of interest on the way, whether historical, geological or even mythical but John's excellent photography is bound to tempt you to every corner of the county. He has trodden every step of the way, experiencing Shropshire in all seasons and conveys his love of this unique and varied landscape in his writing. The original Shropshire Way was a circuit of the Shropshire Hills with a spur to Whitchurch. The new route includes the Meres and Mosses in the north of the county which are areas of Special Scientific Interest. Both loops are centred on Shrewsbury making repeat visits possible if using public transport. The new guide to the Shropshire Way, together with the website, will enable many walkers to discover and enjoy our beautiful county.

With this guide you will be well prepared for your walking holiday in Shropshire. You will know what to take, when to go and how to get there, even if you are one of those who up to now only understands that Shropshire is over west and somewhere near Wales. What a treat you have in store!

*Audrey Menhinick*
*Chairman of Shropshire Way*
*Association*

*https://shropshireway.org.uk*

# ROUTE SUMMARY TABLE

| Stage | | Distance | Ascent | Time | Page |
|---|---|---|---|---|---|
| 1 | Shrewsbury to Bridges | 14¾ miles (23.8km) | 535m | 7hr | 32 |
| 2 | Bridges to Bishop's Castle | 11½ miles (18.4km) | 585m | 6–7hr | 44 |
| 3 | Bishop's Castle to Clun | 11 miles (17.8km) | 575m | 6–7hr | 53 |
| 4 | Clun to Craven Arms | 11¼ miles (18km) | 515m | 6hr | 62 |
| 5 | Craven Arms to Ludlow | 10¾ miles (17.4km) | 340m | 6hr | 69 |
| 6 | Ludlow to Wheathill | 10¼ miles (16.5km) | 630m | 6hr | 76 |
| 7 | Wheathill to Wilderhope Manor | 11¼ miles (18.3km) | 495m | 5–6hr | 83 |
| 8 | Wilderhope to Ironbridge | 12½ miles (20.1km) | 390m | 6hr | 91 |
| 9 | Ironbridge to Wellington | 11 miles (17.6km) | 705m | 6hr | 99 |
| 10 | Wellington to Haughmond | 11¾ miles (19km) | 150m | 6hr | 106 |
| *10A* | *Haughmond to Shrewsbury Link* | *5¼ miles (8.3km)* | *45m* | *2½hr* | 112 |
| 11 | Haughmond to Wem | 11¾ miles (18.9km) | 160m | 6hr | 117 |
| 12 | Wem to Ellesmere | 14½ miles (23.4km) | 120m | 6hr | 126 |
| *12A* | *Wem to Whitchurch* | *14½ miles (23.4km)* | *120m* | *7hr* | 134 |
| 13 | Ellesmere to Llanymynech | 14 miles (22.4km) | 90m | 6hr | 144 |
| 14 | Llanymynech to Nesscliffe | 14¼ miles (23km) | 140m | 6hr | 150 |
| 15 | Nesscliffe to Shrewsbury | 12 miles (19.4km) | 165m | 5–6hr | 158 |
| **Total** | | **182 miles (295km)** | **5760m** | **99hr–103hr** | |

*Totals do not include the Whitchurch leg or the Shrewsbury link*

*Half-timbered houses at Much Wenlock*

# INTRODUCTION

*A dry Montgomery Canal near Pant*

Shropshire has been blessed with some of England's most serene rural beauty, from its colourful red earth, which adds a richness to the pastures and cliffs, to sleek escarpments, rocky outcrops and verdant pastured ridges in the south and its wide plains and charming sleepy villages in the north. In between, the River Severn slithers and meanders like a serpent on its long journey from mountain to sea.

Poets and artists over the centuries have eulogised about the county, including Wilfred Owen, Mary Webb and DH Lawrence. In *A Shropshire Lad*, AE Housman wrote:

> In valleys of springs of rivers
> By Ony and Teme and Clun,
> The country for easy livers,
> The quietest under the sun

And Shropshire as a whole is quiet and peaceful, with only two big towns: Shrewsbury and Telford. Others, such as Whitchurch, Ludlow, Bishop's Castle and Bridgnorth, are small but very pleasant market towns, many with a violent and colourful past, for Shropshire borders Wales and has often fallen to the Celtic princes from the west. Ruined castles in all corners of the county and Offa's Dyke on the western border are a testament to this past.

## THE SHROPSHIRE WAY

The original Shropshire Way was conceived by local Ramblers Association groups in 1978 to link Cheshire's Sandstone Trail with the Offa's Dyke

15

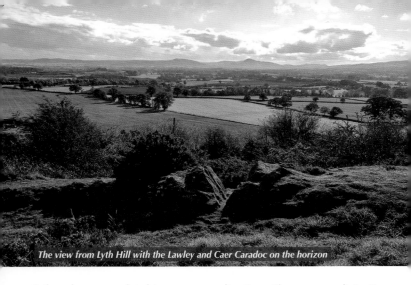

*The view from Lyth Hill with the Lawley and Caer Caradoc on the horizon*

Path and was completed two years later. The route in the first guide by Robert Kirk had a northern extension from Wem to Grindley Brook near Whitchurch and routes through Shrewsbury to Bridges, onwards over the Long Mynd to Ludlow and back to Wem via the Clee Hills, Wenlock Edge, Ironbridge and the Wrekin. The circular was complemented by a Clun extension via Offa's Dyke, taking in Stiperstones and a little section of Offa's Dyke.

Between 1991 and 1995 the route was updated and became a 140-mile circular based on Shrewsbury, but still with the northern extension to Grinshill. Unfortunately, in the 2000s the route gained 32 different loops and followers were sometimes confronted by signposts with the Shropshire Way pointing in three or four different directions. There was no distinction between loops and the main route on the 'buzzard' waymarkers.

In 2015 at the Shrewsbury Ramblers AGM proposals were made to identify a single main route and to re-form the Shropshire Way Association. After consultation a new 180-mile circular route (200 miles including the Whitchurch leg) based on Shrewsbury was devised using the best of the loops in the north, visiting Llanymynech, Ellesmere, Whixall and Wem and retaining the Sandstone Trail link to Grindley Brook. The southern route used the Clun extension rather than the shorter Long Mynd route. A Shrewsbury link was added for those who wanted either a north or a south circular route.

The Shropshire Way visits much of the county's best countryside, although, by its nature as a county circular way, it cannot go everywhere. The hills of Stretton, including the Long Mynd and Caer Caradoc, have been omitted in favour of the Wrekin, the Stiperstones, the Offa's Dyke borderlands and Wenlock Edge.

Shrewsbury, with an impressive castle, over 650 listed buildings and the lovely River Severn, makes a fine start to the walk and the Shropshire Way finds an ingenious route through green sylvan corridors out into the countryside to the south. Little Lyth Hill serves as a taster for things to come as the Shropshire Way enters the Shropshire Hills Area of Outstanding National Beauty (AONB). At day's end you come down through the lovely Golden Valley to Bridges, a tiny community with an inn and a hostel, sheltered in folds between the Long Mynd and Stiperstones. Stiperstones, a fine ridge of heather bilberry and jagged splintered tors, comes early the next day, with the fascinating offbeat little town of Bishop's Castle coming at the end.

On the following day the Way flirts with the Offa's Dyke path for a while and descends a beautiful grassy ridge, the Cefns, to its conclusion at the medieval castle town of Clun. Two days of undulating hillside, woodland and riverside paths brings you to the south of the county at Ludlow, described by John Betjeman as 'Probably the loveliest town in England'. Here, the once

powerful castle town with fine Tudor and Georgian buildings overlooks the rivers Teme and Corve. In the background there's an interesting rakish escarpment known as Titterstone Clee Hill, which will be the highlight of the next day. Although it's been ravaged by quarrying and has masts and a couple of radomes sticking out from the summit, this is a fascinating place with a view of most of the Midland plains and the Welsh hills. The same can be said of Brown Clee Hill, the highest place in Shropshire.

Wenlock Edge provides easy limestone ridge-walking for half a day before the descent into Ironbridge, birthplace of the Industrial Revolution. This fascinating place deserves an extra day, so, if you're thinking about having a rest day, make it here.

The iconic Wrekin provides the last real hill of the walk, although there will be a few small sandstone hills in the next couple of days. From Haughmond, where there's a fine old abbey, you have the choice of curtailing the route and heading back on the 5-mile trek to Shrewsbury or doing the longer route around the plains of northern Shropshire. The northern route explores the market town of Wem and visits the mosses and meres around Whixall and Ellesmere. Canal towpaths aid progress and take you to Llanymynech, a little town straddling the Welsh–English border.

A grassy flood embankment known as the Argie, which runs parallel to the River Vyrnwy, leads the route back eastwards, always in the shadow of the distinctive peaks of the Breidden Hills. The very last small sandstone hill comes at Nesscliffe, where you can see a highwayman's cave and huge red quarry cliffs. The last day is easy and highlighted by the pretty village of Shrawardine and a lovely walk back to Shrewsbury by the banks of the Severn.

For the readers who want to discover those missing hills, the Stretton Skyline Walk has been added: a challenging 19½-mile (31.4km) itinerary taking in the Long Mynd, Ragleth Hill, the Hope Bowdler Hills, Caer Caradoc and the Lawley. For those who prefer an easier schedule, this walk could be completed over two days with Church Stretton providing an ideal breaking point to stop overnight.

## SHROPSHIRE'S HISTORY

The first known settlement in Shropshire is at the Roveries near Lydham, just north of Bishop's Castle. Although the fort is Iron Age, evidence has been found of a Neolithic (Stone Age) settlement dating back to before 2000BC. Shropshire, like most of England at this time, was heavily afforested and the Stone Age people forged highways such as the Portway across the region, erected stone circles and standing stones and buried their dead in raised barrows (tumuli) on the 'open' ridges. Axes and other flint tools have been found all over the county. The first evidence of tree

clearing comes from the people of the Bronze Age (2000BC to 800BC).

In the Iron Age period (800BC to AD43) the Celts put down roots and began to construct hilltop forts and settlements with roundhouses. Examples of these on the Shropshire Way include the forts topping the Wrekin, Bury Ditches and Nesscliffe. In Shropshire the Cornovii tribe ruled and probably had their capital on the Wrekin Hillfort. The tribe cleared large swaths of the valley woodland into fields where they grew cereals, peas, beans and cabbages.

The Cornovii were here when the Romans came to the area in AD47. They were led at this time by Virico. The Romans, under Governor Aulus Plautius, attacked the Wrekin fort and eventually overpowered it but Virico must have put up a good fight for the Romans named their city at nearby Wroxeter Viroconium (sometimes known as Uriconium) in honour of their enemy. The conquerors rapidly built forts of their own and roads such as Watling Street to link them. The Cornovii disappeared into history.

After the Romans abandoned Britain in the fourth century much of what we call Shropshire today became the Welsh Kingdom of Powys and later Pengwern. These border grounds were the scenes of many a battle. In 656 the region was overrun by Saxons and became part of Mercia. In 765 the Mercian King Offa built Watt's Dyke to repel the Welsh. He then advanced with his troops to take Shrewsbury

*Ludlow Castle*

before driving them back into the hills. By 779 he had constructed the Offa's Dyke earthwork border between Chepstow and Prestatyn.

King Edward the Elder merged Mercia into his kingdom of Wessex. The Danes made many forays into the region, mostly unsuccessful or short-lived. They succeeded in destroying the original Wenlock Priory but were eventually driven out by Edward. In 1006 England was divided into shires and Scrobbesbyrigscire (Shropshire) was born.

When the Normans conquered England in 1066 Wild Edric, a Saxon nobleman, owned much of Shropshire. He fought hard to repel the enemy but eventually had to surrender to William the Conqueror. Much of the land, including Shrewsbury, was ceded to Roger de Montgomerie. Over the next two centuries powerful castles were built at Shrewsbury, Ludlow, Clun, Bridgnorth and Bishop's Castle. Many monasteries and abbeys were built at this time, including those at Shrewsbury, Haughmond, Much Wenlock and Buildwas. Scrobbesbyrigscire became Salopescira, which is the origin of Salop.

There were frequent skirmishes between the Plantagenet kings and their Norman barons. At this time the Welsh were making inroads into the county again, with Prince Rhys flattening Clun Castle and Prince Llewelyn the Great taking Shrewsbury Castle. In 1216 King John took the castles of Clun and Oswestry only to have John Fitz-Alan, an ancestor to the Dukes of Norfolk, take them back. In revenge King John had Oswestry burned to the ground and took Clun once more.

The Percy Rebellion against Henry IV concluded at the Battle of Shrewsbury in 1403, when the Lancastrian king defeated Henry Percy (Harry Hotspur) of Northumberland. The battle was immortalised by William Shakespeare's play *Henry IV*.

By the late 14th century Ludlow had over 1100 inhabitants and had become one of the more powerful towns in England. In 1472 Edward IV founded the Council of the Marches, whose power was centred at Ludlow Castle. The council presided over much of Wales and the counties of the English Marches.

In Tudor times Shropshire's population doubled and it developed a vibrant economy. Shrewsbury became an important cattle market at this time, and the wool and cloth trade flourished, while the navigable River Severn became crucial to transportation of the goods.

The people of Shropshire were largely Royalists. At the beginning of the Civil War in 1642 King Charles I visited Shrewsbury and Wellington, where he made the Declaration of Wellington, promising to uphold Protestantism, the laws of the country and the liberty of Parliament. Shrewsbury was forced to surrender in 1644, and the Royalist strongholds of Ludlow and Bridgnorth were captured in 1646. In 1689 the Council of the Marches was suspended and Ludlow's importance waned.

The 18th century brought the Industrial Revolution. Coalbrookdale in the Severn Valley is generally regarded as its birthplace. In 1708 Abraham Darby leased the Coalbrookdale furnace and started iron-smelting with coke. John Wilkinson, a precision engineer of Broseley, built cylinders for early steam engines and also produced the first iron boat.

Under instructions from Abraham Darby III, Thomas Pritchard designed the first cast iron bridge in 1779 to link the important industrial towns of Broseley and Madeley in a place now known as Ironbridge. The 30-metre bridge, which has recently been repaired, still spans the Severn to this day and the two towns became known throughout the world for the production of tiles, clay pipes and bricks. The Ironbridge Gorge Museums (www.ironbridge.org.uk) are a must-see if you're in the area.

The coming of the canals, then the railways accelerated the march of industry; quarrying and mining were now practised on a large scale in order to feed the new industries with raw materials for roads, factories and furnaces.

The New Towns Act of 1946 was passed to disperse population. It gave rise to a plan which would eventually create Shropshire's largest town and one which would re-house people from the slums of Birmingham. The initial scheme of 1963 was to create a new town at Dawley, replacing a derelict area of closed mines and ironworks with houses, roads and

The Iron Bridge at night

schools. In 1968 an amendment order expanded the new town to encompass the Ironbridge Gorge, Oakengates, Shifnal and Wellington. It would be called Telford after the famous engineer, who was at one time Surveyor of Public Works in Shrewsbury. The scheme was supported by the construction of the M54 motorway linking with the M6 near Birmingham, the encouragement of new industries from home and abroad, a new railway station and a huge shopping centre.

## SHROPSHIRE'S GEOLOGY (BY RONALD TURNBULL)

Nowhere else as small as Shropshire has so much geology going on. Within the county, 11 of the 13 geological periods are exposed. The fourth of them, the Silurian Period, was first uncovered along the England–Wales border by Roderick Impey Murchison in the 1830s; it takes its name from the Silures tribe who under Caractacus may (or may not) have fought the Romans at Caer Caradoc. Of the Silurian's four constituent epochs, two (Ludlow and Wenlock) have Shropshire names.

For comparison, the Lake District is made of three basic rock types, of two geological periods. A single Shropshire hill, the Wrekin, has no fewer than eight different rock types, from six separate periods.

### Squashed-up Shropshire

The UK (provided you don't look too closely) has a simplish rock structure. North and west takes you deeper and more ancient: from the clays of London down through the Chalk, the Coal Measures, all the way to the ancient continental crust of the Scottish Highlands. Shropshire compresses most of this sequence into the width of a single county. We will survey the county from its eastern edge, where the most recent rocks form fairly intelligible layers.

The top (youngest) rocks here are from the Triassic and Permian periods. This 'New Red Sandstone' forms no notable hills, but Shropshire's north-eastern lowlands. It is seen as the pale brown Grinshill Stone used in the handsome buildings of Bridgnorth, Shrewsbury and Wellington.

Next down in the sequence, and next west in the county, the

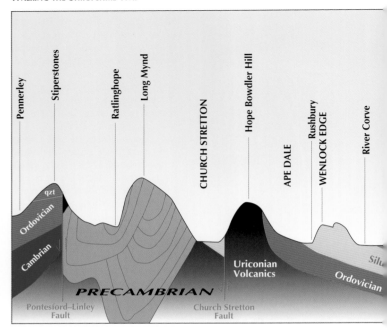

Carboniferous Period formed the Coal Measures at Ironbridge; and also the tops of all three Clee Hills, with old bellpit workings on top of Abdon Burf.

Below the Carboniferous lies the Old Red Sandstone. It forms the lower slopes of the Clee hills, and down into Corve Dale; the reddish stone was quarried at the beautifully named Devil's Mouthpiece.

**Below the old red sandstone**
These Devonian-Age sandstones form a thick, featureless and almost fossil-free layer across the kingdom. For the early geologists, 'below the ORS' meant rocks that were deep, twisted, ancient and mystifying. It was in the Wye Valley and in Shropshire that Roderick Impey Murchison started to make sense of what he would name as the Silurian Period.

Wenlock Edge and Hoar Edge show knobbly reef structures and layered sea-floor limestone; some beds are made up of small tubular crinoid (sea-lily) fragments. Patches such as nylon dish-scrubber are ancient coral. Shells are also common.

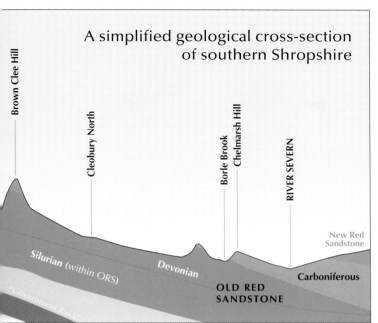

A simplified geological cross-section of southern Shropshire

Brown Clee Hill

Cleobury North

Borle Brook

Chelmarsh Hill

RIVER SEVERN

New Red Sandstone

Silurian (within ORS)

Devonian

Carboniferous

OLD RED SANDSTONE

"Government Rock"

For casual fossil hunters, best places to look are fresh scree and stream pebbles around Wenlock Edge. But also keep eyes open in villages, especially old drystone walls, for shells and for the wiggly lines that were worm burrows.

### Church Stretton crumple zone
Down to the west from Wenlock, there's just space to squeeze in the Ordovician Period, around Cardington at the base of Caer Caradoc. And then we arrive into the Church Stretton crumple zone.

*Old Red Sandstone at Grinshill (Stage 11)*

Here rocks of the earliest geological periods, Ordovician and Cambrian, are embedded within crumpled and mashed ancient crust stretching back into the Precambrian.

Ordovician rocks pop back up as the tottering towers of Stiperstones. The ancient earth movements have tilted it almost upright; after 500 million years of hard times, the stones have just been broken up a bit more by freeze-thaw of the Ice Age.

Even older stones, from the Precambrian, make the Long Mynd's grey-to-black sandstone. It is folded and tilted almost vertical in the rocky stream hollows running down to Church Stretton.

The great Church Stretton fault, running southwest towards Ludlow and northeast to Newport, has not only moved rockforms sideways past one another but it has also moved them up and down. To the west of the valley and its railway line, ancient rocks have been moved downwards; east of the line, everything has moved up. And so the very old grey sandstones of the Long Mynd look across Church Stretton towards even older, and quite different, volcanic rocks of Hope Bowdler Hill and the Lawley.

### Volcanoes of Uriconia

Uriconium Cornoviorum was the Roman town on the site now occupied by Wroxeter. The Uriconian Volcanics started off as a chain of volcanic islands, which were then crushed and mangled up in a continental collision. So Wrekin and Earl's Hill, Caer Caradoc, Lawley and Hope Bowdler Hill have the same origin as Lakeland or Snowdonia, albeit 100 million years earlier. And these rugged hills east of the Stretton valley show the same mix of black basalt, grey andesite and pale grey to pink rhyolite; the same sort of lava flows and volcanic ash that make Snowdon or Scafell.

Scrambled Shropshire is difficult indeed when it comes to puzzling out how the various rock types fit together. But, by the same token, these small hills are a superb sampler of a dozen sorts of stone, from sea-floor coral and limestone of Wenlock Edge through the white quartzite Stiperstones, to the volcanic ash of Caer Caradoc and the ancient mangled crust that makes the Long Mynd.

### WILDLIFE AND PLANTS

Common heather or ling grows prolifically over the acidic soils of the Stiperstones, while bell heather thrives on the drier, sunnier hillsides. The heathers are often interspersed with bilberry, known as whinberry throughout the county. The Stiperstones has cowberry and crowberry too. Red grouse are common on the heather moors, as are ravens and buzzards and the blackbird-like ring ouzel can be found here too, along with skylarks, meadow pipits and redstarts. Red kites have been thriving here too after their re-introduction to

the area. Well-camouflaged grayling butterflies can be found on the heath, along with green hairstreaks and emperor moths.

Mat grass, which is so unpalatable to sheep, is found on poor acidic grounds of the Clee Hills. Wenlock Edge and the hills around Oswestry are of limestone, often ravaged by quarrying and mining. Here, herbs such as wild thyme, wild basil and marjoram flourish. On or near the coppiced woodlands of Wenlock Edge you will see not only bluebells and garlic but herb Paris, violets, the yellow bird's-nest, primroses and orchids, including quite rare bee orchids.

In the north, the raised peat bogs of Whixall and Bettisfield are a haven for the rare Waved and Fork-mosses. You will also be able to see insect-eating sundew, adders, if you're ever so quiet, and water voles, if you're lucky and even quieter.

## WHEN TO GO

You can walk in Shropshire at any time. Winter, when the snow has fallen on the higher ground, gives the hills a new dimension and most sogginess in the ground will be replaced by a crunch underfoot. When the sun is out, the atmosphere is often crystal clear and you can see for 50 miles in every direction. Some of the vegetation will have died back making progress along the paths easier. Woodland paths may however be slippery at this time.

Spring is a delightful time when nature is vibrant with new life and colour. The bracken is still red. In the woods the vivid chrome green of the new leaves contrasts with the abundant spring flowers that have poked their heads up above last year's leaves. If it has been wet over winter, the paths across farmland and in the woods may still be muddy.

In summer, when the days have lengthened, the ground will have dried out, although some low-level paths may be overgrown with nettles and occasionally common hogweed. Make sure you take your waterproof leggings at this time for dew-drenched vegetation can soak you quite quickly as can farmers' crops, which might well be tall at this time. Mid to late August is the best time to see the heather blooming on the Stiperstones.

In autumn the nights draw in again but the flame-colours of the bracken and the woods add great beauty to the landscape. Bilberry leaves have turned red and the heather to dark russet. Together they mix with the grasses to create a tapestry of colour any tweed designer would be proud of.

## GETTING THERE

### Bus
National Express (www.national express.com) has a service (410) which runs from London to Shrewsbury via Birmingham and Telford.

### Trains
Shrewsbury has a mainline station mostly served by KeolisAmey Trains, which run direct services from South Wales, Manchester, Holyhead, Birmingham and Chester. The Transport for Wales website (https://tfwrail.wales) provides times of trains, prices and a booking facility.

## GETTING AROUND
Regular rail services link Whitchurch, Wem and Shrewsbury; Wellington and Shrewsbury, also Ludlow, Craven Arms and Shrewsbury. Buses between stages can be difficult in the more rural areas, although a useful bus links Whitchurch, Wem, Grinshill, Hadnall and Shrewsbury, which is very useful if you're doing the northern section in stages. Regular buses also link Shrewsbury with Craven Arms and Ludlow. For more transport information for getting around the county, see Appendix C.

## ACCOMMODATION AND PLANNING
Appendix B contains a fairly comprehensive list of stage-by-stage accommodations but this will go out of date so it's always best to check websites such as www.booking.com or www.trivago.co.uk when planning your overnight stays. The Shropshire Way Association intends to provide an up-to-date accommodation list too: https://shropshireway.org.uk.

Shrewsbury and Ludlow have accommodation of all types, so finding something suitable will usually be relatively easy unless a major event is taking place. The same cannot be said of rural Shropshire and you should book well in advance. While campers have more flexibility, if you intend to spend the night in a hotel or B&B it is advisable to book well ahead and book the accommodation in chronological (ie stage) order. The stages between Ludlow and Wilderhope are particularly difficult and may involve a taxi ride to and from your stage ending. I have provided a selective list of taxis in Appendix C.

The 15 stages in the book (see the route summary table in Appendix A) make a relatively easy itinerary for anything outside the winter months but the fittest walkers could probably manage to do Ludlow to Wilderhope in one day. Clun to Ludlow would also be a possibility. This would reduce the route to 12 days, which would mean fitting the walk within a two-week holiday.

Being a circular route, walkers could start anywhere but transport links favour Shrewsbury, the book's main starting point. That said, Ludlow, Wellington and Whitchurch have railway stations and reasonable bus routes. The last-mentioned would make a good choice for those who want to undertake the complete circular route plus the Whitchurch leg. The Whitchurch leg has been written in both directions to facilitate this.

If holidays are limited the route can be done stage by stage using public transport – check Appendix C for more information. If you're parking a car at one end it is better to take the bus, train or taxi ride at the beginning and walk back to the car. Shropshire has a good network of footpaths and bridleways so it does lend itself to circular walks. It would be feasible to walk half a section of the Shropshire Way and return using an alternative route: for instance, you could walk north on the Shropshire Way over Brown Clee Hill and return on the Jack Mytton Way. In the north, you could discover more of those meres and mosses around Ellesmere.

*Bridges Youth Hostel (Stage 1)*

## SAFETY

Although nowhere in Shropshire is really remote it is extremely important that all walkers are fully equipped and practised in the use of map and compass. If bad weather such as a blizzard comes in quickly then trouble can occur in a matter of minutes.

Make sure to take enough food and water and keep additional emergency rations in the corner of the rucksack. Not taking enough food is the quickest way of becoming tired; being tired is the quickest way of sustaining an injury. Good breathable waterproofs are essential, as getting cold and wet will render the walker vulnerable to hypothermia.

## WHAT TO TAKE

What you take depends on how you're going to tackle the Shropshire Way. If you're camping you'll need additional gear: a tent, sleeping bags, a carry mat, cooking stove and utensils; if you're hostelling you may need a sleeping bag.

**The basics**
- a quality rucksack: 35 litre or more if staying in B&Bs, and 55 litre or more for backpacking
- liner or plastic carrier bags to keep your gear dry inside the rucksack
- breathable waterproofs, both jackets and trousers
- good proven waterproof boots
- walking socks

- fleece jacket or warm sweater
- changes of clothes for evening wear
- sun hat and sun cream (outside winter months)
- first-aid kit (including plasters for blisters)
- whistle and torch in case of emergencies
- mobile phone (but be aware that there are many 'no reception' areas in rural Shropshire)
- food and plenty of fluids for the day
- maps and guidebook.

**Optional**
- a GPS unit or GPS app and maps for your smartphone.

## USING GPS

In recent years GPS units such as Garmin, Memory Map and Satmap have become quite sophisticated and now they usually include OS mapping for the UK. They are a very useful addition to your equipment, especially if you're caught out in hill fog on the mountains.

In addition to the dedicated GPS units there are apps for iPhones, Android and Blackberry smartphones and tablets too. Viewranger and Memory Map are the best known and their maps are stored on your phone rather than being 'in the cloud' (like Trailzilla maps). The obvious drawback being that if the maps are in the cloud and you don't have a phone signal, then you don't have a map.

Most dedicated GPS units come with map packages. Some come with complete OS Landranger 1:50,000 maps for the UK, while others just include national parks. OS Explorer maps are better and you can buy DVDs or USB sticks with the complete UK, although they are more expensive. The other way of doing this is by going online and downloading and paying for the exact area you want (Memory Map and Viewranger both enable this). You can always add to the area you bought later.

All units will need charging at the end of the day. Dedicated GPS units can usually last at least eight hours and most have facilities to attach battery cases to keep them topped up.

The batteries in smartphones are smaller and most won't last all day when used as a GPS – you'll need at least a 5000mAh battery for all-day use. Otherwise, you may need at least one spare battery or you'll have to use the one you have sparingly, ie, when you're unsure of where to go next. Tablets such as the iPad Mini and Android 7-inch ones usually have larger batteries and can be kept in waterproof cases that can hang around your neck, in the same way as map cases do. Aquapac do a fine range of such cases. The tablets have the advantage of showing you large areas of the map at once.

If you cannot get to a power source to recharge your unit you can buy portable chargers. A 12000mAh EasyAcc, for example, will recharge an iPhone three or four times or an iPad Mini twice before it needs recharging itself. To clarify things mAh stands for milli-Ampere hour, a measure of a battery's energy storage capacity – the higher the mAh figure the better. A word of caution here: these units should be used as a supplement to the maps – the battery may lose power unexpectedly.

## WAYMARKING

The Shropshire Way is well-signed throughout, with orange waymarkers featuring a buzzard and small black arrowhead pointing in the direction of travel. More historical black and white waymarkers can still be seen in places, including the ones marking old alternative loops. In a very few places these appear to contradict the new waymarkers. In such cases always follow the line marked by the orange waymarkers.

*Shropshire Way waymarker*

## USING THIS GUIDE

The Shropshire Way can be completed in one large circular route but by using the Haughmond to Shrewsbury link route described in Section 10A it can be split into both southern and northern circulars. To these ends, the link route has been described in both directions.

All places mentioned in the text are shown in **bold** if they appear on the maps. The box at the start of each walk lists information such as: the distance of the stage, the height gain, the approximate time to allow, the terrain and places for refreshment, and map used (Appendix A summarises some of this information in table form). While the guide uses OS Landranger maps (1:50,000), which are fine for the mountain sections, they are not as detailed as the OS 1:25,000 Explorer maps, so I would recommend that you take the following OS Explorer maps:

• 201 Knighton and Presteigne
• 203 Ludlow Tenbury Wells and Cleobury Mortimer
• 216 Welshpool and Montgomery
• 217 The Long Mynd and Wenlock Edge
• 218 The Wyre Forest and Kidderminster

• 240 Oswestry
• 241 Shrewsbury
• 242 Telford and Ironbridge
• 257 Crewe and Nantwich (if including the Whitchurch leg)

Also bear in mind the following:
The sections north of Shrewsbury are all relatively new. If you are using printed maps make sure they have data post 2018. If the copies of the maps you buy are older they may have either the wrong routes or, in the case of the north, no route at all.

The current 2018 Harvey Map of the Shropshire Way shows only the old southern sections of the route but they may well update it in the future so it's worth checking.

### GPX tracks

GPX tracks for the routes in this guidebook are available to download free at www.cicerone.co.uk/1008/GPX. A GPS device is an excellent aid to navigation, but you should also carry a map and compass and know how to use them. GPX files are provided in good faith, but neither the author nor the publisher accepts responsibility for their accuracy.

# THE SHROPSHIRE WAY

*Bury Ditches Iron Age fort (Stage 4)*

# STAGE 1
*Shrewsbury to Bridges*

| | |
|---|---|
| **Start** | Kingsland Bridge, Shrewsbury |
| **Finish** | Bridges Youth Hostel, Ratlinghope |
| **Distance** | 14¾ miles (23.8km) |
| **Ascent** | 535m |
| **Descent** | 330m |
| **Time** | 7hr |
| **Terrain** | Town streets, woodland and field paths, two ridge tracks |
| **Map** | OS Explorer 241 and 216 |
| **Supplies** | Shrewsbury, Bayston Hill |

Looking at the map the first day doesn't promise much but, in reality, it offers many pleasant surprises in small packages. Shrewsbury is an historic delight and the way out, through the Rad Brook and Rae Brook valleys, gives walkers more greenery and beauty than they have the right to expect in the suburbs of a sizeable town. Then there's Lyth Hill with its airy ridge, its blossoms and its wide panoramas.

The Shropshire Way begins to climb in earnest late in the day with the ascent of Wilderley Hill and it follows the course of the ancient Portway. By now the iconic Stiperstones tors have come into full view. The day is ended with a very pretty descent into the Golden Valley where the path weaves between grassy folds in the hills down to Ratlinghope.

## SHREWSBURY

Although it might have been the site of Pengwern, an early capital of pre-Roman Powys, Shrewsbury, or Scrobbesbyrig as it was then known, was developed as a town in Saxon times, probably around the eighth century and under the rule of Mercia. Previously the largest settlement was the Roman town of Viroconium Cornoviorum (Wroxeter) about 5 miles away, but Roman artefacts have been found in Shrewsbury proving that they would have had some form of settlement here. The town was strategically sited within a tight loop on the river.

Three years after the Norman Conquest of 1066, William I had a primitive timber castle built but this was burned down by Welsh invaders. Roger de Montgomery, a relative of William I, was made Earl of Shrewsbury and he built a more powerful castle on the mound where the current castle lies. The abbey was founded in 1083 as part of a Benedictine monastery and town walls were built in this period and Shrewsbury became the county town of Shropshire. The town fell to Llewelyn the Great, Prince of Wales, in 1215 and it would be a Welsh frontier town for nearly 70 years. In 1283 Edward I, the scourge of the Welsh, had Dafydd ap Gruyffydd tried and found guilty of high treason at Shrewsbury. This last Welsh Prince of Wales was subsequently hung, drawn and quartered. Edward would make his son Prince of Wales thus ending the Welsh dynasty.

In 1403 Henry IV defeated Henry Percy (Harry Hotspur) at the Battle of Shrewsbury, which featured in Shakespeare's *Henry IV* Part 1. You can visit the site at Battlefield in the north-east part of the town.

In the Middle Ages Shrewsbury grew into a sizeable town, its wealth largely coming from the wool trade. Many of the beautiful half-timbered buildings that grace the town today were built in Tudor times. The town centre still retains its medieval street pattern with numerous narrow passages known as shuts. Henry VIII is said to have offered Shrewsbury cathedral city status, something that the townsfolk declined.

The public library sited beneath the castle was built in 1552 as Shrewsbury School. Pupils included the 'hanging judge' Judge Jeffreys and Charles Darwin. The school was moved to its present site at Kingsland in 1882. The sandstone castle you see today was built in 1643 and further repaired with additions, including Laura's Tower by Thomas Telford in 1780. Telford, who at this time was Surveyor of Public Works in Shropshire, oversaw the building of the original A5 London to Holyhead road, which crossed the English Bridge. Many of the monastic buildings of Shrewsbury Abbey were demolished in the process. The A5 now by-passes Shrewsbury.

The railways came to Shrewsbury in 1848. The station buildings were built from stone quarried at nearby Grinshill – you'll see it later on the northern part of the 'Way'. The classical mock-Tudor Victorian building has a fine castellated and pinnacled clocktower.

Today, Shrewsbury has over 650 listed historical buildings. As its industries declined, this rich heritage, along with its beautiful position on the River Severn loop, has enabled the town to flourish as a place of tourism and leisure.

### Getting to Kingsland Bridge

Many Shropshire Wayfarers will be coming from the railway station so the description starts from here, and the route will take in as many of the town's sights as can be fitted into a logical course to the official start on Kingsland Bridge.

With your back to the railway station entrance turn left along **Castle Gates**, past the Bulls Head pub, then the impressive **library** with its statue of Charles Darwin. The castle lies to the left and it would be worth a visit if there's time; otherwise continue to the High Cross, where

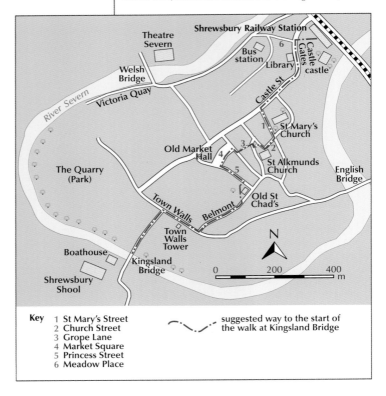

Key   1 St Mary's Street
      2 Church Street
      3 Grope Lane
      4 Market Square
      5 Princess Street
      6 Meadow Place

suggested way to the start of the walk at Kingsland Bridge

the street ahead becomes pedestrianised and where you should turn left along St Mary's Street. This passes **St Mary's Church**, which has Saxon origins.

> The now redundant **St Mary's Church** is maintained by the Churches Conservation Trust. It has one of the tallest spires in England and the interior with the nave's oak ceiling and its wonderful stained-glass windows should be a must-see on your itinerary.

Turn right on Church Street by the Loggerheads pub to reach **St Alkmund's Church**. Turn right, then left on a paved street along the perimeter of the churchyard before descending the Bear Steps, which lie in a passageway through the half-timbered Bear Steps Gallery building. These lead down to Fish Street, where there are several more of the Bear Steps' historic half-timbered buildings. Turn right for a few paces along the narrow, cobbled street, then left down Grope Lane, one of Shrewsbury's 'shuts'. This brings the route onto High Street where you should turn right to the Square. ▶ Pass to the left of both before turning left along Princess Street. On reaching a raised church green, that of **Old St Chad's**, turn right, then turn left along the passageway by the church.

Here you'll see a statue of Clive of India and the Old Market Hall.

> **Old St Chad's** was once a substantial square-towered church but by the late 18th-century it had fallen into disrepair, a fact noted by engineer Thomas Telford, who advised restoration. The church collapsed in 1788 and was largely demolished with only the Lady Chapel and crypt remaining. It was rebuilt as a neo-classical round church overlooking the Quarry Park.

Turn right along the narrow street (Belmont) and follow it to the junction with **Town Walls**. You'll see the old town walls to the left overlooking sports fields. Turn right to pass the 14th-century **Town Walls Tower**, then turn left by Shrewsbury High School. The road leads to Kingsland Bridge. ▶

If you've walked along the riverbank to get here you'll have to walk along a passage on the east side to get on the bridge by Shrewsbury High School.

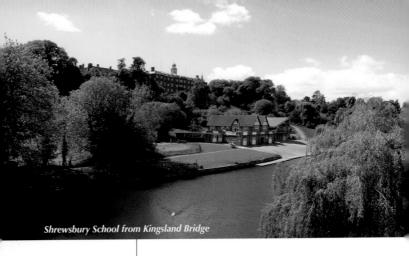

*Shrewsbury School from Kingsland Bridge*

The grand brick-built building high above the opposite bank of the River Severn is that of the 'new' Shrewsbury School.

### Official start of the Shropshire Way

◄ Cross the **Kingsland Bridge** and follow the winding Kingsland Road beyond to a T-junction, where you turn left, then right along Beehive Lane. Beyond the houses this transforms into a stony track through trees and bushes. Turn left at the next junction to cross a bridge over Rad Brook. The path comes out to a road opposite a **cemetery**.

Turn right along the road, ignoring the next right fork (Old Roman Road). Turn left at a busy roundabout, crossing to the pavement on the far side as soon as possible. A Shropshire Way signpost highlights the path along the edge of the school's playing fields in **Meole Brace** and alongside the road.

Novelist and poet **Mary Webb** (1881–1927) grew up in the village of Meole Brace. Holy Trinity church on the roadside to the left is where she and Henry Webb were married. Mary was known for her poetic descriptions of nature and landscape and her first published novel *Golden Arrow* took inspiration from her new home in Pontesbury. *Precious Bane*, a novel from 1924, won her the Prix Femina Vie Heureuse, a French literary prize. After a life of ill health Mary died at the age of 46.

Bear right as the route pulls alongside a railway line, then cross the tracks with care at the next footpath sign. A hedge-lined ginnel then takes the route between houses to a road. Turn left here, then right along a busier road. Turn left again by a vicarage and along Church Road. This passes a small recreation area on the right and Holy Trinity church on the left, where the road turns right, eventually to pass Meole Brace primary school. A little further on, the path forks left by some railings to enter the woods of the Rae Brook Valley.

The **Rae Brook Valley** is managed by Shropshire Council as a local nature reserve, which stretches from the Abbey Foregate almost to the A5. This green corridor through an urban environment is a mixture of streamside woodland and pastureland. Otters and kingfishers are said to live here. In medieval times the valley was farmed by the monks from the abbey. In later years until its closure in 1963 the Severn Valley railway line to Ironbridge and Bridgnorth forged its way through here.

After crossing two footbridges, the second over Rae Brook, take the right fork path between metal railings, then follow the Shropshire Way signs highlighting a short field-edge route leading to a busy road where you should turn right. This takes the Way over a bridge spanning the busy A5 dual-carriageway.

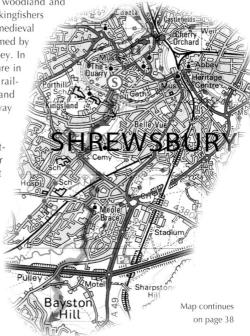

Map continues
on page 38

37

Over the bridge, go through a kissing gate on the left and cross a field to a country lane at **Pulley**. Turn right, passing Pulley House, before turning left through a gate and following the left edge of the first field. Beyond a stile at the far end, turn right by the hedge on the right. Turn left with the hedge to a large tree, where a waymarker shows the way right (southwest) across a large field. The houses of

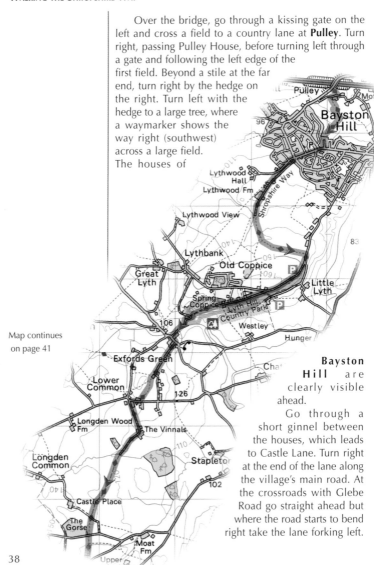

Map continues on page 41

**Bayston Hill** are clearly visible ahead.

Go through a short ginnel between the houses, which leads to Castle Lane. Turn right at the end of the lane along the village's main road. At the crossroads with Glebe Road go straight ahead but where the road starts to bend right take the lane forking left.

Leave the lane at a tarred parking area, keeping to the left of a youth centre building. The enclosed path passes some allotments. Watch out for a waymarked left turn onto a farm lane that takes the route through **Lythwood Farm**. This gradually curves left across huge fields. Where it ends, aim for the left side of a covered reservoir at the far end of the field.

## LYTH HILL

Lyth Hill in blossom

Although it is less than 170m above sea level, Lyth Hill, the first real hill on the walk, offers superb views over the surrounding hills and plains of Shropshire. Looking north among chequered pastures of grass, cereal crops and the odd bright gold of rape are the spires and rooftops of Shrewsbury, framed by the bold outlines of the Wrekin and the hills of the Welsh border. To the east the ridges of Lawley and Caer Caradoc dominate. The serrated outline of the Stiperstones lying to the southwest offers a promise of the day to come.

Three hundred years ago flax and hemp ropes for ships, mines and factories were built here and exported all over the world.

Spring Cottage on the edge of the hill was once home to Mary Webb and her husband Henry. After their separation and in ill health she returned to the cottage. She died in the same year.

39

Turn right along the lane then at the **Lyth Hill car park** take the track on the right. This rises along the crest of the hill.

The most beautiful part of the path descends and rakes along the southern side of the ridge, across slopes where gorse, broom and bluebells thrive alongside fruit trees. It continues through the trees of **Spring Coppice**, which were planted to commemorate the Queen's Jubilee.

By a red-bricked dwelling take the left fork lane and follow it down to a junction, where you turn left, then right on an unsurfaced lane leading to **Exfords Green**. Where the lane turns left at a hedge-lined junction by a farm, take the farm track on the right, then almost immediately follow a waymarked path on the right, passing pens and enclosures. Go through a gate into a field and aim half-left to follow the hedge on the left side. At the far end an enclosed path over a stile leads out to the road near Little Vinnals.

Turn right along the road and left along a farm track by the Hollies (cottage). At **The Vinnals** (farm) go through the farmyard and turn right on a stone and dirt track. Where the track fords a stream, use the footbridge on the right.

Beyond the stream and what can be a muddy area, the Shropshire Way continues along a hedge-lined green lane. Cross the track from **Castle Place** and head south across a field towards the woodland of **The Gorse**. The route meets a country lane at a kissing gate just to the left of the woodland perimeter. Go through the kissing gate on the far side of the lane and continue south across a field. Go across a footbridge at the halfway point before coming out at another country lane with the ongoing footpath staggered to the right beyond another gate. The cross-field path follows field-edges on the left and crosses the first of two footbridges. Keep the bungalow of Cottage Farm well to the left as you cross the next field towards the second footbridge which is slightly obscured by trees but is left of a farm gate. Across this, head for a lane-side kissing gate to the right of the outbuildings of the farm.

Turn right along the narrow lane lined with grass banks and tall hedges. After 1½ miles the lane comes to **Wilderley Hall**, where you turn left on a farm track to start a long, steady climb. The track soon degenerates to a grass track before entering fields. Cross a farm drive linking the Beeches and Sheppen Fields.

In the next field follow a curved grassy bank to a kissing gate at the far side. This cuts a corner from the route shown on current OS maps and is the landowner's preferred route.

Ignore a vague left fork but follow a faint track roughly parallel with the hedge on the right, aiming for the right edge of a conifer plantation. The continuing path follows

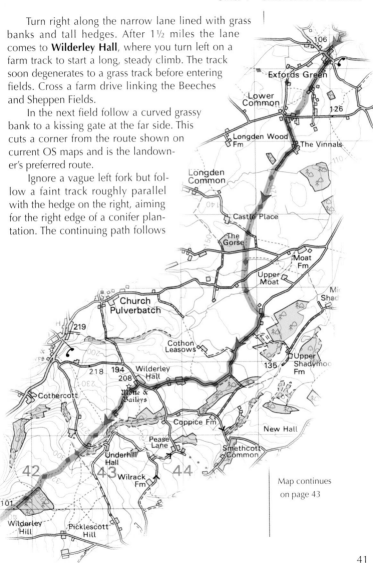

Map continues
on page 43

You'll have noticed a fine if small rugged craggy hill to the north. This is Earl's Hill, which has an ancient fort on the summit.

the edge of the plantation. It soon becomes a wide grassy track climbing **Wilderley Hill**. ◄

From the hilltop continue southwest through a kissing gate in a hedge not shown on the current OS map, then across two fields. In the second field there is a standing stone to your right as you reach a roadside kissing gate. Go straight ahead across the road on a tarred lane, which is part of the Port Way.

**The Port Way** in an ancient track linking the Kerry Ridgeway at the River Onny, south of the Long Mynd and the Wrekin-Oswestry track. It used high ground wherever possible to avoid densely wooded, marshy valleys. The numerous barrows alongside the route are from the Bronze and Iron ages. In medieval times the Port Way later served as a drovers' route between the markets of Bishop's Castle and Shrewsbury.

After a short distance the tarmac surface becomes crumbled and there are views into the Golden Valley of Darnford Brook, with the crag-serrated ridge of Stiperstones on the horizon. Your peace may be disturbed by the sound of trail bikes on the Picklescott Enduro Track on the left. Go through a kissing gate on the right, descending the clear path signed 'to Bridges and Stiperstones'. The path winds through folds of pastured hills, past the renovated farm of Lower Darnford and passing close to the houses of **Ratlinghope**. Finally, it enters pretty woodland, emerging on the lane east of **Bridges Youth Hostel**. ▶

For those staying at the Bridges Inn (formerly the Horseshoe Inn), continue down the road to the first junction and turn left.

The impressive Gothic-looking **Bridges Youth Hostel**, complete with bell tower, was commissioned in 1866 by Lady Scott as a village school but soon closed as there were not enough children in the Ratlinghope area to keep it going. It became a youth hostel in 1931 and remained part of the YHA until 1991 when it became a privately owned hostel. The name Bridges refers to the three bridges over Darnford Brook and the East Onny.

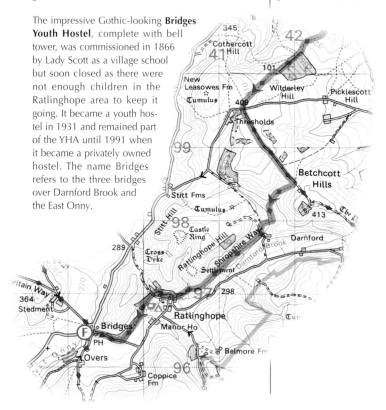

# STAGE 2
*Bridges to Bishop's Castle*

| | |
|---|---|
| **Start** | Bridges Youth Hostel, Ratlinghope |
| **Finish** | Bishop's Castle Town Hall |
| **Distance** | 11½ miles (18.4km) |
| **Ascent** | 585m |
| **Descent** | 630m |
| **Time** | 6–7hr |
| **Terrain** | Country lane, boulder and grassy ridges, field paths |
| **Map** | OS Explorer 216 |
| **Supplies** | Bishop's Castle, and there's a café ½ mile off route at the Bog Centre |

Yesterday, although the Way had a taste of the hills on the Port Way, it traversed relatively gentle and pastoral landscapes. Today, country lanes lined by hedgerow and flower-decked grass verges lead the route to one of Shropshire's most iconic ridges, that of the Stiperstones. Here great jagged tors protrude from heather slopes tempting the would-be climber to scale their mini summits. The Way then deposits its followers back into the valley before whisking them back up to the heights of Linley Hill. Here a gentle decline on a grassy ridge leads to the fields of the West Onny Valley. Just one short climb and a gentle descent away lies Bishop's Castle, a small, quirky town with a fascinating history.

From **Bridges Youth Hostel** follow the lane westwards to the junction by the Bridges Inn. Turn right along the lane climbing above the inn's car park, then go left at the road junction signed 'Wentnor, Norbury and Bishop's Castle'. After 50 metres turn right on the lane signed 'Stiperstones National Nature Reserve'. Beyond the Stedment farm complex take the right fork. The quiet lane threads through pastured hills with the spiky tors of Stiperstones dominating the view ahead. It curves to the right and after 1¼ miles is abandoned for an even narrower lane leading up to **The Hollies** (farm), beyond which a track continues in the same direction before bending right.

Fork left soon afterwards, up to a gate in the top right-hand corner of the field. The track then climbs further to a gate at the edge of the moor. Go through this and take the left fork track, which climbs towards the ridge.

On reaching the 'crossroads' of tracks turn left along the ridge path of **Stiperstones** through the heather. This soon becomes studded with quartzite rocks, making fast progress slightly more difficult. The path climbs through heather and bilberry to the impressive jagged crest known as the **Devil's Chair**, then onwards to the conical

Map continues
on page 49

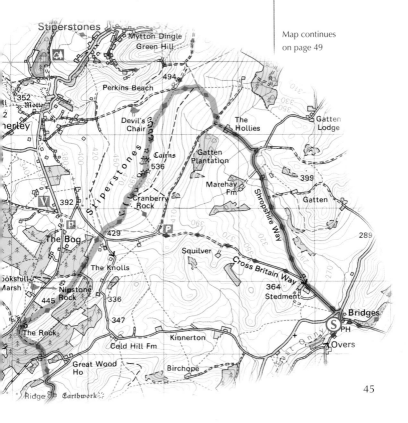

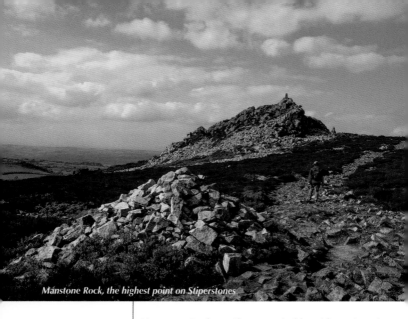

*Manstone Rock, the highest point on Stiperstones*

Manstone Rock, easily recognisable with a trig point crowning its summit.

## STIPERSTONES' SUMMIT

Nearly 500 million years ago the mountain's summit ridge would have been rising out above glaciers. The ground was subjected to constant freezing and thawing, which shattered the rock into the screes and tors you see today.

Views from the ridge are tremendous. The prominent hill a few miles away to the southwest is Corndon Hill, which leads the eye to the more distant hills of Mid Wales, the most prominent being the Berwyn mountains. To the east the elegantly smooth ridge of the Long Mynd stretches out from beyond the chequered pastures and golden wheat fields of the East Onny Valley.

The path now descends through more heather, but the main 'highway' forking left should be abandoned for a narrow trod that stays with the ridge, passing **Cranberry Rock**. The ridge has an abundance of cowberry, crowberry and whinberry, but cranberry isn't among them.

Beyond Cranberry Rock the path descends south-westwards to a gate at the edge of the access area. An enclosed grass path leads the way through a gate onto a country lane, which should be crossed to go through a gate on the far side. Continue in the same direction across fields, keeping the buildings of Upper Knolls Farm well to the left. The path then enters a conifer plantation (note: some of the trees were being felled around the path in 2018) before coming out again on the open hillsides of the **Nipstone Rock Local Nature Reserve**.

At one time Stiperstones and Nipstone were smoth-ered with coniferous forest but the Shropshire Wildlife Trust, English Nature (now Natural England) and the Forestry Commission started a scheme known as **'Back to Purple'**, whose aim was to restore the heather moorland. The conifer plantations at Nipstone were felled between 2001 and 2006, replaced with more natural oaks, ash and rowan. The heather and bilberry are back, as are the views across the heathland ridges. You can see skylarks, meadow pipits, emperor moths and, in season, eat the whinberries.

The path comes to a junction of wide tracks with the view dominated by the twin crags of Nipstone Rock. The Shropshire Way goes straight ahead, by-passing the rocks but if you want to climb to the top turn right along a wide track leading towards a car park. Just before you get there, go over a step-stile on the left-hand side, beyond which a narrow path leads to the top. Once you have scaled the rocks look for a narrow trod on their southeast-ern side. This takes the route back to the wider path used by the Shropshire Way. ▶

There's a shooting club at Brooks Hill to the west, so you may well hear gunfire.

The path narrows and descends to the right of the next crag, known simply as **The Rock**. It meets a wide grass track, where you turn left, descending between a boulderfield beneath The Rock and a conifer plantation.

Ignore the left turn path beyond a gate but instead descend towards woodland ahead down to a lane. Turn right then, after a few paces, go over a stile on the left and descend a pasture, passing over a plank footbridge over a dyke, then another one across a stream. Beyond this a mud path climbs steeply through woods to reach another lane, where you turn right. Just beyond **Ridge Farm** go through a farm gate on the left (the second of two) – it is signed the Shropshire Way.

A track from the gate follows a hedge on the left, then arcs right to reach the top of the field. Beyond a large tree the 'Way' goes over a stile by a farm gate and follows the left edge of a coniferous wood – not the nearby rutted farm track – and continues towards the ridge on Linley Hill. Go through a gate in the fence on the right (a few metres below the ridge) and then angle up the hill to go right alongside the ridge fence.

Through the next gate take the right fork route along **Linley Hill**. The ridge gradually descends to a long avenue of ancient beeches. ◄

The beeches, planted around 1815 to commemorate the British victory in the Napoleonic Wars, are reaching the end of their life but new ones are being planted to take their place.

*Ancient beeches on Linley Hill*

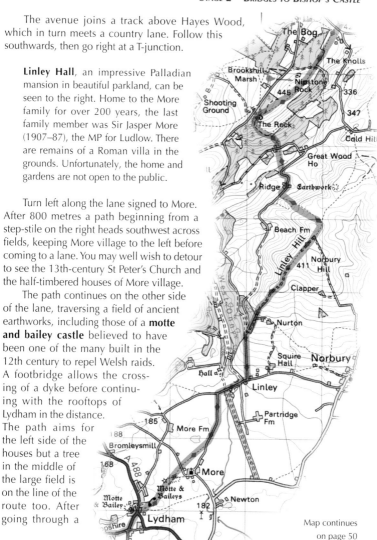

The avenue joins a track above Hayes Wood, which in turn meets a country lane. Follow this southwards, then go right at a T-junction.

**Linley Hall**, an impressive Palladian mansion in beautiful parkland, can be seen to the right. Home to the More family for over 200 years, the last family member was Sir Jasper More (1907–87), the MP for Ludlow. There are remains of a Roman villa in the grounds. Unfortunately, the home and gardens are not open to the public.

Turn left along the lane signed to More. After 800 metres a path beginning from a step-stile on the right heads southwest across fields, keeping More village to the left before coming to a lane. You may well wish to detour to see the 13th-century St Peter's Church and the half-timbered houses of More village.

The path continues on the other side of the lane, traversing a field of ancient earthworks, including those of a **motte and bailey castle** believed to have been one of the many built in the 12th century to repel Welsh raids. A footbridge allows the crossing of a dyke before continuing with the rooftops of Lydham in the distance. The path aims for the left side of the houses but a tree in the middle of the large field is on the line of the route too. After going through a

Map continues on page 50

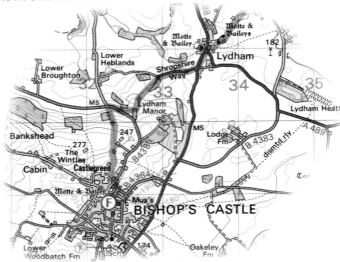

kissing gate the path emerges by the village hall car park in **Lydham**.

Turn left along the main road before taking the right fork Bishop's Castle (A488) road. After 250 metres turn right along a stony farm track. Where this veers right go straight ahead, through a small gate next to double gates, and climb across the field towards the forest on the left. Go through a gate into the forest onto a path that traces its northwestern perimeter.

On leaving the forest the Way continues, enclosed at first, but later along the right edge of a field. Watch out for a fingerpost surrounded by bushes and trees on the right. This points the Way right through the trees, across a small field and out to a B-road near the farm of Upper Heblands. Turn right along the road and follow it to the first junction. Go over a stile on the left and climb past a forest on the right. In the next field the Way comes across the Foxholes Campsite (not marked on current maps) and is diverted left from the route shown on 2017 OS maps along a stony track into the complex. After a few paces the path leaves the track and turns right through a gate. In the next large field, it rejoins the proper route and descends towards the rooftops of Bishop's Castle.

At the bottom end of the field the route continues along a tree-lined path. After crossing a track on the edge of the village the path exits by a gate to a passageway between houses before turning right along B4385 road at **Castle Green**. Follow the B-road as it curves left beyond a crossroads, then turn right along Bull Street which leads to the Market Square in the centre of **Bishop's Castle**.

## BISHOP'S CASTLE

Bishop's Castle lies 200m above sea level, sheltered from the west winds by a hollow among the hills. The main street, which begins as Church Street and continues as High Street, climbs in fine style from the church to the Market Square above the town hall. It's lined by many historic buildings, some painted in bright colours with ornate designs. You may notice that the clock on St John the Baptist's Church has no minute hand and hasn't had since as long as townsfolk can remember. Opposite the church is the 17th-century Six Bells pub and microbrewery, while on Salop Street, just off the High Street, is the oldest brewery in United Kingdom, the Three Tuns Brewery, which was licensed in 1642 and continues to produce real ale to this day.

Much of the town you'll see today is Georgian, but there are many fine Tudor houses at the top end of High Street. The Old Time Gallery is one of the oldest. Behind the town hall is the half-timbered House on Crutches, an Elizabethan building housing a museum, which tells the story of this remarkable town.

In the eighth-century the manor of Lydbury North, which included what we now know as Bishop's Castle, was owned by Egwin Shakehead, so called because of his affliction with trembling palsy. He was miraculously cured following a visit to the shrine of Saint Ethelbert in Hereford Cathedral and being eternally grateful gifted the estate to the Bishop of Hereford.

After the Norman Conquest of 1066 the area became troubled by skirmishes with the Welsh. The Bishops of Hereford were appointed as Marcher Lords, responsible for the protection of the Marches, the frontier lands between England and Wales. At this time a motte and bailey castle, one of many, was founded and a town grew below it. By the late 13th century, the name Bishop's Castle appeared in official documents. King John bestowed a

*Historically rich Bishop's Castle*

market charter in 1249 and a bustling town of many inns became a stop-off point for cattle drovers, who would have been herding cattle to and from Wales using the Kerry Ridgeway drove road.

By the 17th century, records show that the castle was derelict, stripped of its lead and masonry, much of which was used to build new houses. Today you can only see the scant remains of one of the castle walls. During the 18th and 19th centuries the town was one of England's notorious 'Rotten Boroughs', where the rich and powerful bought votes to ensure their favoured candidates were elected to Parliament. The Walcotts, who had bought the borough from Queen Elizabeth I in 1573 and had held the lands ever since, were caught up in the scandal. They sold up to Robert Clive, better known as Clive of India, who probably perpetuated the wrongdoings. The Reform Act of 1832 ended all this and, like the other 55 rotten boroughs, the town hasn't had its own MP.

# STAGE 3
## Bishop's Castle to Clun

| | |
|---|---|
| **Start** | Bishop's Castle Town Hall |
| **Finish** | The Square, Clun |
| **Distance** | 11 miles (17.8km) |
| **Ascent** | 575m |
| **Descent** | 595m |
| **Time** | 6–7hr |
| **Terrain** | Village streets and lanes, grassy ridges and field paths |
| **Map** | OS Explorer 216 Welshpool and 201 |
| **Supplies** | Bishop's Castle and Clun |

Today, the 'Way' discovers Offa's Dyke and silky green landscapes that could do Ireland proud. If you didn't look around the town yesterday, to do so this morning would be a good idea – most of the sights are on the way downhill to the church. Beyond the town the Way begins on a fine track that heads south across pastured hillsides, then follows the delightful valley of Wood Batch. The climb up Colebatch Hill offers beautiful retrospective views of Bishop's Castle and the Kerry Hills. After flirting with the wooded Unk Valley at Churchtown, the Shropshire Way joins forces with the Offa's Dyke Path, taking an undulating course by the earthworks of the Dyke to Hergan, where they part. Our route takes in the grassy ridge of Cefns and follows it down to Clun Castle.

From the town hall in **Bishop's Castle**, head downhill, past all the Tudor and Georgian buildings to the square-towered St John the Baptist's Church. At the T-junction in front of the church, turn right, then left up Church Lane past the fire station. Go right by Field Lane, then left on a signed stony Shropshire Way track heading south. Beyond some cottages, go straight ahead through a farm gate onto an unsurfaced green lane across high fields. The route is joined briefly by a stony farm lane. Where that turns left keep straight ahead alongside a hedge on the left. ▶

By now many forest-topped hills feature in a verdant pastoral landscape.

The Way draws level with the village of **Colebatch** and descends pastured slopes towards a stream. At the very foot of the slopes turn right along a faint path, roughly following the river.

After crossing many stiles and a footbridge over a side stream, the path comes to a pretty hedge-lined country lane, where you should turn left. The lane crosses the stream, then swings right by **Wood House** (farm) and terminates on the approach to Middle Woodbatch Farm (B&B and campsite). Follow the succeeding drive uphill and between the farm buildings.

Just beyond the buildings turn off the track through a waymarked gate on the left. A narrower tree-lined mud and stone track climbs the hillside to emerge on high pastures on the shoulder of Colebatch Hill. ◀

*Looking back, you'll see a lovely view of Bishop's Castle and the Long Mynd.*

Follow the fence on the right, then at a Shropshire Way waymarker, turn left uphill to a visible gate on the horizon. On reaching and going through the gate turn right, following the hedge and fence along the edge of the field, past an old barn to a country lane. Turn left along the lane, then right on a beautiful tree-lined, rutted grass and

Map continues on page 56

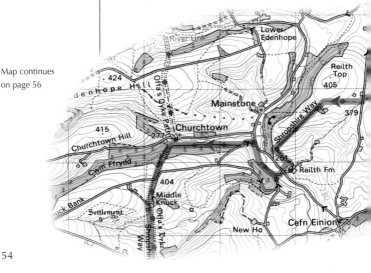

*View back to Bishop's Castle from the shoulder of Colebatch Hill*

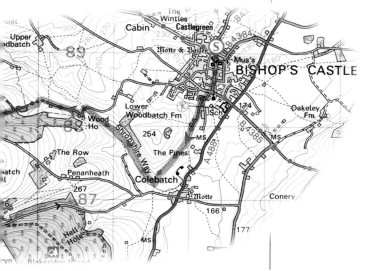

Map continues
on page 58

stone track
known as
Reilth Mynd.
Where the track
turns left to the large
house (Fron), go straight ahead on a sunken grass track,
which descends towards the Unk Valley.

Where the track curves left, descending towards
**Reilth Farm**, go straight ahead to the corner of a large
field before turning left with the hedge. Just as you meet
the track abandoned earlier turn right through a waymarked gate and follow the hedge-lined grass path down
to a junction of country lanes.

Go straight ahead and over the bridge across the
River Unk. Immediately beyond, take the path on the
right, which traverses the lower edge of Knuck Wood.
After leaving the wood behind the path cuts diagonally
across a sloping field, keeping to the right of the cottage
on the far side. This leads to a lane-side stile.

Turn left along the lane, then left again at a junction, past the cottage and up the hill. Fork right on a path

beyond a gate to trace the lower edge of Churchtown Wood. ▶

The path soon turns left, steeply uphill. You may have noticed earthwork banks on the left, slightly obscured by the trees. You have joined the **Offa's Dyke** long-distance footpath and it is the ancient dyke you're walking beside.

**Offa's Dyke** was built under Saxon rule. While Wales had little need for political borders, for Wales had hills, the English border kingdoms in general did not. By the middle of the eighth century King Offa of Mercia had extended England's borders as far as Northumberland and Wessex and felt the need to reinforce the border with the Welsh. The dyke they built had an earthwork wall up to 2.4m high and a flanking ditch. It spanned the borderlands from Chepstow on the Bristol Channel to Prestatyn on the North Wales Coast.

You'll see the pretty little chapel-like St John's Church through the trees. That's all there is to Churchtown, which in reality is an outlier to the parish of Mainstone.

*Walking beside Offa's Dyke*

The path crosses a road before continuing alongside the dyke. It descends into a wooded coombe before climbing gently to cross a farm lane at **Middle Knuck**, now a Keys care/activity centre. Climb to a gate beyond the complex and keep to the right of the barn. After descending briefly once more to cross a stream beneath Eaton's Coppice, which doesn't seem to have the trees marked on the map, the path climbs towards the grassy hill ahead known as **Hergan**.

The Offa's Dyke and Shropshire Way routes part company just before a roadside beneath Hergan. The Shropshire Way turns left on a wide track climbing over the shoulder of the hill, passing sheep pens and a quarry en route. Where the track ends, a waymarker highlights the direction across the field to a stile in a fence (SO 267 855). The path now runs alongside a fence and line of trees on the left before descending to **Three Gates** (farm) through a little hedge and scrub-enclosed ginnel and over a stile to a country lane.

On reaching the lane, keep straight ahead, following the 'Bicton and Clun' sign. Just beyond another farm and where the road bends left, go straight ahead along what can be a muddy farm track climbing towards Cefns (Cefn means ridge in Welsh).

Where the farm track ends continue the climb with a hedge on the right. Beyond the next stile a narrow trod angles slightly left to climb to the top left corner of the field – the ridge-top, close to the summit of the **Cefns**. The glorious, free-striding path will now follow the hedge along the spine of the ridge.

> From the **summit of Cefns**, panoramic views open up to reveal the valleys of the Unk and Clun. The village of Whitcott Keysett appears in the valley on the right, then Clun Castle can be seen in the distance towering above the rooftops of the town but dwarfed by the slopes of the conifer-clad Black Hill behind it.

The route down the ridge is highlighted by numerous stiles but at all times the route is obvious. The path becomes enclosed by trees and shrubs and descends to a muddy cross-track. The onward path here is staggered to the left and will follow a fence and hedge on the right. At the far end of this next field you'll see a little rock summit on the left. Beyond the next stile, the right of way takes a slight shortcut across a field then rejoins the field-edge on the right and follows it to the lane at the bottom.

The continuing path lies immediately opposite on the far side of the lane. Here, go over a stile by a gate and follow a mostly hedge-enclosed path gradually curving left to head ESE towards the River Unk. On reaching the riverbank the path follows it closely with a hedge now to the left. Eventually it crosses on a footbridge before following a track, which soon joins a surfaced lane leading past pretty cottages. Where the lane turns left go straight ahead through a gate onto a path that skirts the east side of **Clun Castle**.

As the route comes to a stile by the castle entrance turn left to the road. Unless you are continuing your journey to the youth hostel (that would be straight ahead along Newport Street and left at its end) turn right

## CLUN

Clun Castle

AE Housman described the border town of Clun as the quietest place under the sun in his book, *A Shropshire Lad* and so it is, being far away from the cities in a rural corner of Shropshire.

Known in Welsh as Colunwy, Clun developed by a seventh-century Saxon Church on the south side of the river that shares its name. At the time of the Norman Conquest of 1066 it was under the rule of the Anglo-Saxon noble Eadric the Wild (Wild Edric). Eadric resisted the Normans but was eventually defeated and his lands were confiscated.

Norman baron, Picot de Say, built a motte and bailey castle here in the middle of the 12th century as Clun became a Marcher Lordship in its own right. The castle was burned to the ground in 1196 by Lord Rhys, a powerful Welsh leader, but the walls were rebuilt in stone by the FitzAlans, the Earls of Arundel. The castle included a 25m-tall keep known as the Great Tower, which strangely sits aside the main castle mound. The town on the north side of the river was developed at this time. The castle was built to keep out the Welsh but it failed to do so again in the early 15th century, when Owain Glyndwr destroyed it and overran the town. The castle, although managed by English Heritage, is owned by the Duke of Norfolk, a descendant of the FitzAlans.

From medieval times Clun was a stop-off on a drove road between the markets of the Midlands, mid Wales and London. In 1450 the current pack-horse bridge was built across the river. The five-arched stone bridge still carries the main road through the town, although heavy vehicles have to divert to avoid it.

The grave of playwright and actor, John Osborne (1929–94), who wrote *Look Back in Anger* among many other works, lies by the path in St George's churchyard.

along Enfield Street to the Square, where there is a post office/general store and the popular White Horse Inn. The Sun Inn and the Maltings Café lie further east along the main street of **Clun**.

# STAGE 4

*Clun to Craven Arms*

| | |
|---|---|
| **Start** | The Square, Clun |
| **Finish** | Shropshire Hills Discovery Centre, Craven Arms |
| **Distance** | 11¼ miles (18km) |
| **Ascent** | 515m |
| **Descent** | 580m |
| **Time** | 6hr |
| **Terrain** | Country lane, forest tracks, grassy hills, woodland and field paths |
| **Map** | OS Explorer 201, 216 and 217 |
| **Supplies** | Clun and Craven Arms |

It's sad to say goodbye to Clun but there's so much more to see. The day begins on winding country lanes, gradually climbing towards afforested hills. The forests, when encountered, turn out to be rather pleasant with far more broadleaved trees than conifer, and with less formal forestry tracks than the norm. The highlight of the day comes early, for those forest tracks lead to the Bury Ditches hillfort, whose earthwork rings, clad with wildflowers and bright yellow broom, make an ideal platform to see far and wide across the Shropshire countryside. Beyond this the 'Way' passes through Walcot Wood, where huge oaks shelter in a narrow, secluded valley. After descending to the ancient village of Hopesay there's a steep but entertaining climb to the top of Hopesay Hill, where you first spy the red rooftops of distant Craven Arms. Paths now traverse a pastoral landscape on an easy-paced finale to the busy little town.

From the Square in **Clun** head north past the post office/shop up Enfield Street. Turn right along Newport Street before turning left at the T-junction and passing the youth hostel. At the first bend beyond the hostel, fork left along a drive before rounding the right side of the house and crossing three fields in a NNE direction, and rejoining the road further north. This comes to the farming hamlet of

**Guilden Down**. Take the right fork lane here and follow it to the Tea on the Way tearoom, where the route turns left onto a tree-lined track that soon enters the forestry plantations. Fortunately, most of the trees you'll see are pleasant broad-leaved ones – the conifers are behind them and out of view.

The forestry path joins a track coming from the left. Maintain direction, staying with the main track until a signed left fork track SO 320 834 takes the route towards **Sunnyhill**. The track eventually doubles back right and circles the slope beneath **Bury Ditches fort**. It soon ends at a gate where you cross the summit and the earthworks of the fort to a gate at the other end. ▶

The path at the other side of the fort heads ENE through the forest, passes to the left of a car park with picnic benches and comes out at a country lane south of a village known as Lower Down.

Indistinct tracks on the left lead to the summit toposcope, where you get the best views.

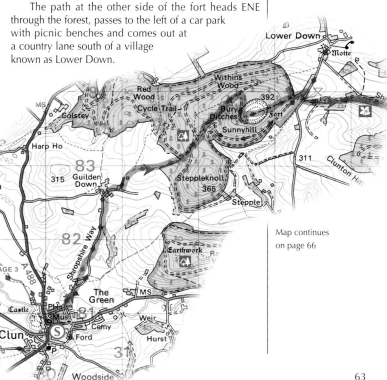

Map continues on page 66

63

## BURY DITCHES

*On Bury Ditches, Iron Age fort*

The settlement of around 2.6ha dates back to about 500BC. Until 1976 it was overplanted with conifers but many of the trees in the higher regions were blown down by a storm. The Forestry Commission felled the remaining stands to reveal an elliptical fort defended by earthwork ramparts and ditches reaching as high as 7m. The ramparts overlap around the western entrance to provide further protection from enemy advances, while the eastern entrance is in-turned, which means the rings turn in to form a passage intended to draw the enemy into a tight space, where they could easily be ambushed. In Bury Ditches' case the passage was 40 metres long. In the Iron Ages the Bury Ditches would have been inhabited by people living in simple round huts within the fortification.

Today the Forestry Commission has waymarked routes around the fort. They have also helped in the conservation of the rare Wood White butterfly, which can be seen here throughout the summer. Windswept long grasses and colourful yellow broom help to emphasise the impressive geometry of the rings.

Turn right along the lane then go left on a farm track, which passes Stanley Cottage before entering Walcot Wood. Fork right on a minor path descending to the streamside before rejoining the main track near Lodge Farm.

## WALCOT WOOD

Once part of the 18,000-acre Walcot Estate initially used as a deer park, Walcot Wood is a small wooded valley enclave shaded from the elements by Clunton Hill and Walcot Park. In 1763 Clive of India bought the estate including the hall, which lies to the north on the other side of the hill.

The trees of the deer park are long gone to limestone pasture. The valley woodlands are now managed by the National Trust. There are over 30 veteran oaks (ones that are over 300 years old – most are much older) in the valley. The holes and crevices in these accommodate many species of animal, also insects, who like the rotting wood. The rare deadwood beetle can be found here.

At certain times of the year, the woods are coloured by the mauve, yellow and white petals of violets, wood sorrel and primroses and by the bluebells too.

At a junction of tracks 1200 metres beyond the Lodge turn right for a few metres then left over a step-stile. This angles left across a small enclosure before heading across a larger field towards a house (there are actually two but one is partially hidden at this stage). Go over a stile onto a track that takes you between the houses. After following their drive go through a kissing gate on the right, which marks the start of a field path heading SSE towards the buildings of Kempton. After crossing the large field, then a small enclosure, the path comes to a track and lane, where you turn left to the road into **Kempton**.

Turn right then left along a tarred lane, which degenerates into a stony track. After 1¼ miles the Shropshire Way leaves the track through a gate on the right and turns immediately left, then right along the perimeter of a field with tree-cloaked Burrow Hill looming large. Go through a gateway at the top end of the field and

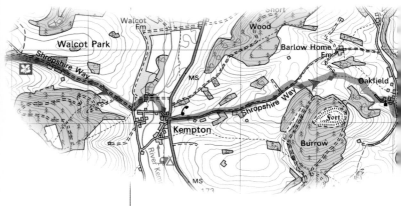

*St Mary's Church, Hopesay*

follow the hedge on the right ENE across two fields to enter another large field south of Bird's Wood (SO 382 836). The field boundary shown as guiding the Way down here doesn't exist but a Shropshire Way finger-post highlights the direction of descent. Soon the path

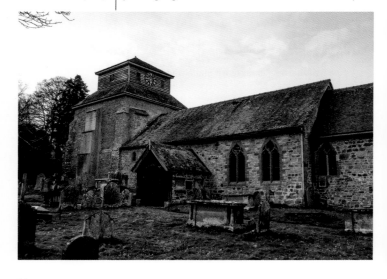

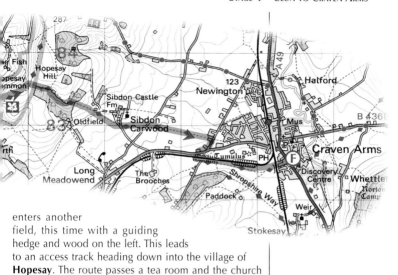

enters another
field, this time with a guiding
hedge and wood on the left. This leads
to an access track heading down into the village of
**Hopesay**. The route passes a tea room and the church
before coming to the road at the bottom. Turn right
along this.

> '**Hopesay**' derives from 'Hope de Say', the valley
> of de Say, a reference to the Norman barons of that
> name, who arrived in Shropshire after the 1066
> invasion and who eventually established and occu-
> pied Clun Castle.
>
> The 13th-century church of St Mary, restored
> around 1880, is a grade I listed building with a
> broad buttressed limestone-rubble tower and a
> 17th-century double-pyramidal roof, known as a
> Montgomery Dovecote. There's a classic Norman
> arch over the South Doorway.

Beyond the last houses turn left through a kissing
gate onto a clear cross-field and woodland path that
heads east and cross a footbridge before climbing to a
kissing gate at the foot of **Hopesay Hill**. A bold grass path
takes the route steeply to the summit. ▶

There is a good view
back across Hopesay
to Burrow Fort –
now you can see
the ruffled outlines
of its earthworks
for the first time.

67

By now you'll be getting glimpses ahead of the red-bricked houses on the outskirts of Craven Arms.

The path continues northeast to a pine plantation on the ridge. Over a stile by a gate, pass along the north side of the plantation. Go over a stile by a farm gate and continue along the fence-line to cross a stile into sloping pastureland. A waymarker highlights the ESE direction of the faint path descending fields down to a cottage, hidden by trees until the end. Go over a stile to the front of the cottage and head south-eastwards down the next field, keeping the hamlet of Sibdon Carwood with its castellated manor house well to the left. ◄

Go through a kissing gate to cross the driveway of **Sibdon Carwood** before heading east across another field path to reach a country lane. After crossing this continue eastwards across the next field. Over a stile turn half-right and follow the line of the hedge on the right. This leads to a new (2017) housing estate. Go through a gate onto a path across a small green, before turning right along a lane. Take the right fork just before meeting the busy Clun B-road. Cross the road and follow the lane ahead to pass beneath a railway bridge. Now turn left on a field path running alongside the Heart of Wales railway line. Maintain direction where the railway curves left. The path, now known as Dodds Lane, goes under the Ludlow line railway bridge, passes through a small housing estate and comes out at the A49 opposite the Shropshire Hills Discovery Centre in **Craven Arms**.

# STAGE 5

*Craven Arms to Ludlow*

| | |
|---|---|
| **Start** | Shropshire Hills Discovery Centre, Craven Arms |
| **Finish** | The Buttercross, Ludlow |
| **Distance** | 10¾ miles (17.4km) |
| **Ascent** | 340m |
| **Descent** | 355m |
| **Time** | 5hr |
| **Terrain** | Country lane, forest tracks, grassy hills, woodland and field paths |
| **Map** | OS Explorer 217 and 203 |
| **Supplies** | Craven Arms (very good Tuffins supermarket), Ludlow |

After you stock up in the bustling little town of Craven Arms, the Shropshire Way will take you across the meadows of the River Onny to historic Stokesay Castle. From there it climbs through woods to the little village of Aldon before tracing two splendid wooded gorges, the Aldon and Brandhill gutters. The middle section is easy, on country lanes and bridleways traversing wide flat fields. There is anticipation as the route closes in on Ludlow, where there's fascinating history around every corner, from the powerful Norman castle to the town gates and the Buttercross, the official centre of Ludlow.

Go around the left side of the discovery centre in **Craven Arms** and follow the main path down the valley, ignoring three paths on the left. The path soon passes through woodland. Where it turns left take the little path forking slightly right and arrive at a gate beside the A49 road – cross with care. Across the road turn left along a tarred path, which leads to the Stokesay Road. Turn right along this, following it past the 12th-century church and **Stokesay Castle**.

The lane comes to a railway level-crossing next to a brick-built house. Cross the tracks with great care and turn left on an old byway. Where the byway forks right

## STOKESAY CASTLE

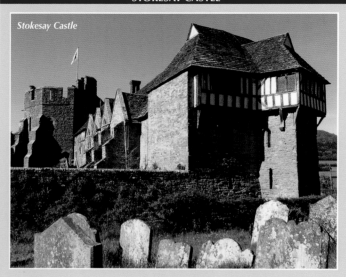

*Stokesay Castle*

This large fortified manor house was built in the late 13th century for wool merchant Laurence of Ludlow. Laurence's descendants would become well established in the region, often serving as Sheriffs of Shropshire. In the late 15th century, the castle was passed by marriage to Thomas Vernon. Unfortunately, his grandson Henry defaulted on huge debts and was sent to Fleet Prison. At the time of the Civil War the castle was in the hands of William, the first Earl of Craven, a known Royalist. The castle was besieged in 1645 and surrendered to the Parliamentary forces. Stokesay was to be 'slighted' but only minor damage was inflicted at this time.

Restoration commenced in the 1830s by William Craven but the Cravens themselves fell on hard times and sold the castle to the wealthy industrial magnate, John Derby Allcroft and, under his tenure, it was lovingly restored but kept empty. It became a popular tourist attraction, which opened to the public in 1908. In 1986 Jewell Magnus-Allcroft put the house under the guardianship of English Heritage and indeed bequeathed the property on her death in 1992.

## STOKESAY ESTATE

Aldon Gutter and Brandhill Gutter are twisting streams that form deep and narrow wooded valleys draining the hills between the Clun and Onny rivers. Before flowing into the Onny they feed the Stonehouse Pools below. All this is part of the Stokesay Estate. On your way down the valley you'll see glimpses of the grand Stokesay Court, built between 1889–92 for John Derby Allcroft who found Stokesay Castle too small for his needs. Unfortunately, Allcroft died six months after its completion. The house became a soldiers' convalescent home during the First World War but its main claim to fame is that it was used as the setting for Tallis House in 'Atonement', the critically-acclaimed Oscar-winning film of 2007.

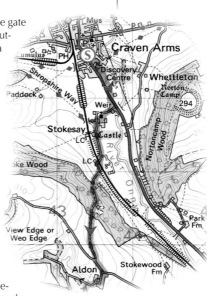

uphill leave it and go through the gate ahead, then turn right along a rutted track climbing uphill by a hedge. Go through the top gate and continue straight ahead along the stony track you just left. This climbs above Stokewood Cottage through pleasant woodland then out to high fields with superb views across to the Clee Hills, Ludlow and the Mortimer Forest. The track ends on a high country lane close to the hamlet of **Aldon**.

Turn left along the lane before turning right in the centre of the hamlet. Just beyond a right-hand bend, 250 metres beyond Oat Mill Barn, leave the lane for a bridleway on the left. This descends into the wooded dene of Aldon Gutter.

As you approach the bottom of the dene, turn right on a little culverted bridge across a dyke then follow the waymarking arrow towards, then behind, the old

Map continues on page 72

The bottom of the dene can be very muddy in winter.

house. ◄ After passing close to some pheasant pens, cross a track onto a bridleway following the south side of Aldon Gutter before winding right into Brandhill Gutter. Watch out for a path to the left, there's a Shropshire Way signpost by a streamlet marking the position of a ford. Once across, take the lower woodland path on the left, which follows the stream back out into Aldon Gutter where it joins a muddy track and follows it past the Stonehouse Pools (reservoirs) and up to a country lane by a wooden barn and outbuildings. Turn right, then take the left fork lane signed to Clungunford.

Follow the lane past the farm of **Wetmore** before turning

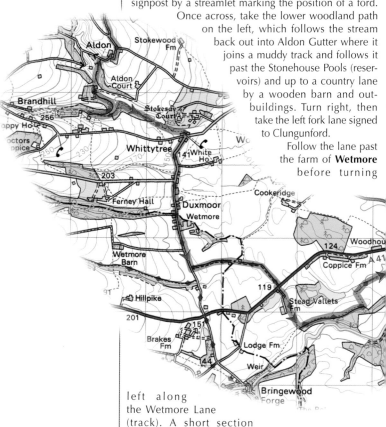

left along the Wetmore Lane (track). A short section beyond Wetmore Cottage degenerates into what can, outside the summer months, become an extremely muddy track. However, things improve beyond Cookeridge

Cottages. The lane comes to the busy A4113 road. Follow the lane, which is staggered to the right across the road, past a stone cottage and the tree-enshrouded Upper Pool.

As the lane turns right towards **Stead Vallets Farm** leave it for a signed footpath on the left which heads SSE by a hedge on the right in a huge crop field. Turn left at the far end of the field and trace the perimeter of the woods of Stocking Nursery. At a Shropshire Way waymarker at the southeast end of the huge field turn left alongside the hedge to reach Lower Pool, where the Way goes right alongside the hedge on the left. Go through the gateway at the end of the field and turn right, soon to join the bankside path of the River Teme.

The village of Bromfield with its square-towered church appears ahead. As the path nears the village it goes over a stile, turns right along a lane and over the three-arched Bromfield Bridge. The long straight tarred lane continues through the manicured estate of **Oakly Park**.

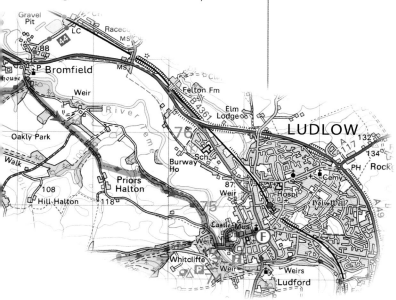

*Dinham Bridge
at Ludlow*

On Mondays,
Wednesdays,
Fridays and
Saturdays, markets
are held here.

Just before reaching Priors Halton the route leaves the lane for a short stretch of farm track on the left. At the end, turn diagonally right (ESE) on a well-waymarked route across fields, then right along the edge of a wood. This leads back onto the lane you left opposite to the Cliffe at Dinham (hotel). Turn left along the lane then cross Dinham Bridge over the River Teme.

Beyond the bridge and the riverside café turn left on the next lane (the Linney), then fork right on a surfaced path that rounds Ludlow Castle's tall outer walls. The path emerges at the castle gates at the end of Castle Street. Continue along the latter. ◄

At the end of Castle Street the road divides. Take the wider High Street, which leads to the Buttercross, an impressive classically designed stone building overlooking Broad Street in the centre of **Ludlow**.

## LUDLOW

Described by John Betjeman as 'the loveliest town in England', Ludlow stands proud on a small hill overlooking the confluence of the rivers Teme and Corve, its church and its great castle forming recognisable landmarks for many miles.

The name Ludlow derives from the old English 'hlud-hlaw', which meant hill by the loud waters – in those days the Teme flowed in quite boisterous rapids. The town wasn't mentioned in the Domesday Book of 1086 but a prehistoric burial mound was discovered and dug up when St Laurence's Church was being extended in 1199.

Construction of the castle began around 1075 for Norman baron, Roger deLacy and during the century that followed St Mary Magdalen's chapel, the Great Tower and the outer bailey were added. The early town was built to a strict plan with wide main streets and narrow side streets.

The town walls were built from 1233 onwards with seven gates. Many sections are evident to this day and quite well preserved. Broad Gate, at the bottom of Broad Street, is the sole surviving medieval gate.

In 1472 Edward IV founded the Council of the Marches, whose power was centred at Ludlow Castle. The council presided over much of Wales and the English Marches but was dissolved in 1689, after which the castle fell into disrepair.

Ludlow held weekly markets for livestock, wool and cloth. Glove-making became a major industry. As these industries declined they were gradually replaced by tourism. This majestic town has 500 listed buildings, including the impressive castle and a cathedral-like church with a 135ft sandstone tower and beautiful stained-glass windows. The church was the final resting place of writer AE Housman, famous for *A Shropshire Lad*. Particularly impressive are the half-timbered Feathers Hotel and the 18th-century Buttercross used as a butter market and council chamber. It now houses Ludlow Museum.

# STAGE 6
*Ludlow to Wheathill*

| | |
|---|---|
| **Start** | The Buttercross, Ludlow |
| **Finish** | Three Horseshoes, Wheathill |
| **Distance** | 10¼ miles (16.5km) |
| **Ascent** | 630m |
| **Descent** | 425m |
| **Time** | 6hr |
| **Terrain** | Country lane, undulating grassland and field paths, moorland |
| **Map** | OS Explorer 203 and 217 |
| **Supplies** | Ludlow |
| **Accommodation** | Currently, there are few options for accommodation on the section to Wheathill (this may change) and it is advisable to plan a taxi ride to get to your chosen B&B. |

The Shropshire Way hits the heights again after a couple of days of modest hill and valley walking. After following the River Teme to the edges of the town the route heads across green pastures to an Iron Age fort at Caynham. The ascent is gentle, across pastures at first, but eventually it traverses fascinating former mining and quarrying country. A grassy tramway incline takes the route past crumbling quarry buildings to the summit of Titterstone Clee Hill, which is topped by white radomes and some rocks known as Giant's Chair. The views are wide and wonderful and are maintained for most of the descent to Wheathill.

With your back to the Buttercross in **Ludlow**, head down Broad Street and under the arch of Broad Gate in the town walls before descending towards the riverbank at Ludford Bridge – don't cross. Turn left on the riverside road, then, where the main road curves left, take the right fork, signed for Bridgnorth and Kidderminster. Turn right again at the whitewashed old toll house to stay by the river. Turn right at the T-junction with New Steventon

Road, which soon becomes a shady, hedge-lined lane. Turn left along the lane signed to Caynham, which takes the route behind the A49 service area (Travelodge and a good Co-op store here). ▶

Turn right at the T-junction with the busy Sheet Road, go across the roundabout, then straight ahead on the road signed to Caynham. After passing through the village of **Sheet** and about 1000 metres from the roundabout, leave the road for a footpath over a stile on the left, descending to cross a water company footbridge spanning Ledwyche Brook. Once over the bridge, head for the wooded hill ahead. A waymarking post in the middle of the field helps you on your way and soon you see an eroded scar of the path ahead. After crossing a rutted track by a cluster of trees go over a stile. The path angles left as it climbs in the next field towards the hill. Over the next stile a discernible path does develop, along that scar you saw earlier and takes the route diagonally up the sides of the hill, through the woodland and onto a circular grassy area. This is **Caynham Camp**.

Planning was passed late in 2018 for a large housing estate to be built either side of the road here.

Map continues on page 79

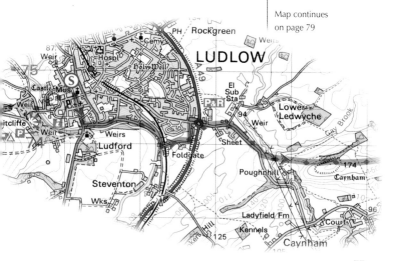

**Caynham Camp** is a univallate (single rampart) Iron Age hillfort of around 4ha. Today the earthwork ramparts are obscured by a ring of trees. Excavations in the 1950s revealed circular houses and granaries. It has been said that there was a medieval castle here but there is no evidence of this. Some historians think it was likely that Cromwell's troops camped here while laying siege to Ludlow in 1646.

Cross the fort top to a passage through the far banks and go over a stile in the apex of the field corner ahead. The route then heads eastwards on a faint waymarked path across three fields. In the fourth the path follows a hedge on the left. The exit stile is staggered to the right. Over this take the left fork path over the next field, across a rutted track at the far end, then over a stile and across a footbridge over a brook (SO 557 739). Climb the bank at the far side and go over another stile. The path continues slightly north of east to cross another footbridge and over a stile at the far end of the field. The next stile lies between two prominent trees at the far corner of the field. From here there's a hedge to guide you and waymarkers on each stile or gate as the path begins to climb northeast. At first the hedge is on the right, but you switch sides (waymarked). The path turns left (north) at a field corner (SO 566 745) using the left one of two farm gates and soon descends to cross a plank footbridge over a streamlet before climbing out to a country lane west of Knowbury.

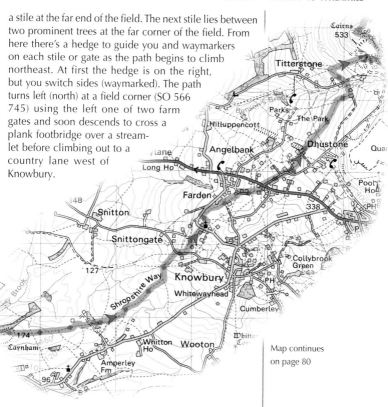

Map continues on page 80

Turn right along the lane before taking the second of two footpaths on the left, which is an enclosed one taking the route up to another lane opposite to the 19th-century square towered stone-built church of St Paul. ▶

An enclosed path continues through a gate on the left side of the graveyard and emerges on a high grassy hillside. The marked route on the map shows the path descending north westwards to the roadside before angling back up to the gate at SO 573 555 but walkers

This was built on land donated by the Honourable Robert Clive (Clive of India).

79

There are views across the rooftops of Farden to the angular Titterstone Clee Hill, with Brown Clee Hill peeping over its shoulder.

have been seen striding freely across the brow of the hill to the same point. ◄ The path now continues northeast across a complex series of small fields with the houses of **Farden** below and left.

Beyond a stable the route comes to a stony lane where you should turn right. Where the lane turns left go straight on along a grassy track, which leads to an open field. Follow the hedge on the left at first but, where this turns left, aim for the left side of the house ahead. Follow its drive to the busy A4117 road.

Go up Dhustone Lane, which is staggered slightly to the left across the highway. This lane goes all the way up to Titterstone Clee's summit but we're not going to take the easy way. At the first right-hand bend, the Shropshire Way turns left on the stony drive signed to nos 4 and 6 Dhustone Lane. Ignore the left turn track but go straight on. Beyond the cattle grid by the last house the Way goes straight on along a mown grass track to a gate and stile on the edge of a field. The path goes diagonally left towards Shop Farm. Keep to the right of the farm buildings and cross the trackbed of an old railway. Maintain your NNE direction across a large field, crossing a farm track en route and keeping the

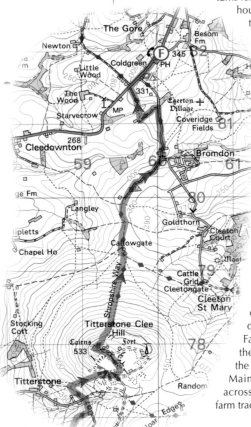

80

next farmhouse some way to the left. Beyond the gate in the far left corner of the field, head northeast on rough ground of rushes and gorse. When you reach a line of wooden electricity pylons follow their line.

Beyond a gate at the end of the rough ground the path follows a hedge on the right with a whitewashed house prominent on the far side. On reaching the far corner of the field the path turns left, descending past the house, before going through a gate leading to the mining and quarrying grounds of **Titterstone**. After descending into a hollow take the track on the left and follow it to the old incline. Climb onto the incline using steps to the left of a bridge and turn right on a steady climb to the mine buildings on a plateau halfway up the hill.

The Shropshire Way path passes to the right of all the buildings before climbing beneath the car park and taking a left fork track to reach the Dhustone Road just beyond the car park. The continuing path forks left from the road and climbs onto the final slopes, bending left to round the top edge of the quarries and passing close to the white radomes. The Shropshire Way bypasses the summit trig point on **Titterstone Clee Hill** and the rocks of the Giant's Chair but it's a short and essential detour to the northwest edge before rejoining the descent route.

*Giant's Chair rocks on Titterstone Clee Hill, looking towards Brown Clee Hill*

## TITTERSTONE CLEE HILL

The third highest hill in Shropshire behind neighbouring Brown Clee Hill and the Stiperstones is formed by a gently inclining line of dolerite sills capping beds of shales and old red sandstone. The complex geology, which includes coal seams and limestone, has led to the hill being ravaged over centuries by quarrymen and miners, mainly for that dolerite, known as Dhustone (Ddu is Welsh for black). At one time over 2000 people worked the hill. Many came from places such as Bridgnorth while others were housed in specially built villages like Bedlam (now re-named Titterstone) on the western slopes and Dhustone to the south. Among the crumbling remains you can still see the narrow-gauge railway incline, although the rails have long gone. The large concrete structure below the car park is where wagons were filled with stone before being transported down the mountain.

Quarrying activities have damaged the Iron Age settlement on the very summit of the mountain, which was the largest of its kind in Shropshire. Part of the ancient wall can be seen on the slope below the cairn – it's a low, spread out line of rocks. There are two Bronze Age cairns and traces of hut circles near the summit. Unfortunately, one of the cairns has been hollowed out to form a wind shelter. The flint tools of Mesolithic hunters found on the slopes of Titterstone show that the area was populated in even earlier times.

More modern intrusions are also to be found on the summit in the form of gleaming white radomes. The larger one controls air traffic for the West Midlands, while the smaller one belongs to the Met Office.

The faint Shropshire Way path descends northeast, then north down a grassy hillslope towards the farm at **Callowgate**. Here an enclosed track known as Callow Lane leads to the road at **Bromdon**. Turn left and follow the road past the farms. Turn left along the drive to the Knapp (farm). ◄ Just short of the farm turn right, descending to a gate and stream, which is culverted at the crossing point. Climb by a field-edge track to Dodshill (farm), where a drive leads out to the B-road at Wheathill. Turn right for the Three Horseshoes pub (where you could have a meal and ring for a taxi) or turn right, then left up the farm lane to Cold Green Barn if you're carrying on.

To visit the Three Horseshoes pub or caravan site you could stay on the road here, then turn right on the B-road at the end.

# STAGE 7
*Wheathill to Wilderhope Manor*

| | |
|---|---|
| **Start** | Three Horseshoes, Wheathill |
| **Finish** | Wilderhope Manor YH |
| **Distance** | 11¼ miles (18.3km) |
| **Ascent** | 495m |
| **Descent** | 580m |
| **Time** | 5–6hr |
| **Terrain** | Country lane, undulating grassland and field paths, moorland |
| **Map** | OS Explorer 217 |
| **Supplies** | None on the route |

Yesterday the 'Way' tackled Shropshire's third highest hill, today it tackles the highest, Brown Clee Hill. From this side Brown Clee is verdant and the way up in spring and summer is beautiful, with the meadows and path-sides decked with colourful wildflowers. Like Titterstone Clee Hill, the summit is a bit industrial but the views are splendid, taking the gaze right into Wales if the atmosphere is clear enough. The way down uses a wonderful sunken green road giving views across the verdant Corve Valley to the limestone country of Wenlock Edge at day's end.

From the Three Horseshoes pub follow the B-road towards Ludlow, then turn right along the lane passing Coldgreen Barn. This descends to cross Coldgreen Dingle before climbing to the farm of **Newton**. Here turn right along a track that comes out at a high lane near **Blackford**.

Go across the lane and follow the track opposite, the unsurfaced tree-enclosed path on the right not the adjacent stony drive. After an unpromising start this delightful hedge and tree-lined track climbs among hillside pastures. ▶

As the path comes to the edge of open hillside it veers left and enters the top regions of Old Lodge Coppice. It

The view back to Titterstone Clee Hill is superb for the sloping hedge-lines rise up to and accentuate the lines of the sleek escarpment's rocky fringe.

Map continues
on page 86

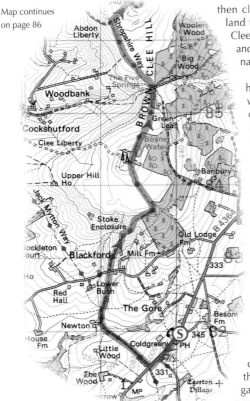

then climbs left across moorland to reach the summit of Clee Burf, topped by a mast and building belonging to a navigational relay station.

The continuing route heads roughly northwards along the ridge of **Brown Clee Hill**, following sheep-tracks 30 metres west of a copse of trees and the ridge fence. It soon becomes more ingrained in the ground and gradually pulls away from the fence-line as it descends towards the saddle separating Brown Clee's two summits. To the west is the verdant pastured hollow of Pole Gutter. You'll also see the impressive earthworks of the Nordy Bank fort.

On reaching the col at **Five Springs** go through the right of two gates ahead. A grass path now heads across the heather and bilberry of Sandy Nap – a fence on the left will act as a guide in poor visibility. ◄

Watch out for the memorial to the 23 airmen killed when their plane crashed into Brown Clee.

Ignore the first rising path on the right – the one by the gate where a path on the other side of the fence joins yours. Instead follow the fence-side path as it continues north with the mast-topped summit on the right. At the next gate (SO 592 863) fork right on a more prominent

## BROWN CLEE HILL

*Looking back to Titterstone Clee Hill from the slopes of Brown Clee Hill*

The highest hill in Shropshire is surprisingly undistinctive from most angles, with only the tall masts making it recognisable from a distance. Like Titterstone Clee Hill to the south, there is a capping of dhustone or dolerite laid down on beds of sandstone with coal measures and limestone present. There were three Iron Age forts, one on Abdon Burf, one on Clee Burf and one on Nordy Bank above Cockshutford. The first two have been destroyed by quarrying activities, the third is intact.

Quarrying and mining dolerite has left its mark on the hill. On this walk you'll come across the stark buildings of the crushing mill and the railway incline that took the stone down the hill in the direction of Ditton Priors. An examination of the topography will also reveal bell pits of the coal industry. The Abdon Burf quarry closed in 1936 and the lower Cockshutford one not long afterwards.

Brown Clee has a history of air crashes. A German Second World War Junkers 88, two Wellington bombers, a Hawker Typhon and a couple of Avro Ansons crashed here and it is believed that the engine and some of the wreckage from one of those Wellingtons lies at the bottom of Boyne Water. Twenty-three Allied and German airmen lost their lives here. These days the radar masts on the Brown Clee and Titterstone Clee hills help pilots avoid such tragedies. The summit is crowned by a trig point and a view indicator. Being the highest point of Shropshire, Brown Clee has uninterrupted views of all the county and its hills, including the Stretton Hills, the Long Mynd and the spiky crest of Stiperstones, with Snowdonia, the Malvern Hills and the Brecon Beacons appearing if conditions are clear enough. To the east across the Wyre Forest, the horizon pales to the flatlands of the Black Country. Nearer to hand you'll be able to see the views over pastoral Corvedale and Wenlock Edge where you may well be spending the night.

track towards the summit masts of **Abdon Burf**, Brown Clee's highest top.

Follow the tarred supply road downhill from the summit, passing the old quarry buildings on the way to the edge of the forest. Here, turn left along the top edge of the plantation, gradually arcing left to its western end. Beyond a farm gate the path continues as a grassy ride on a pastured balcony high above the Corve Valley.

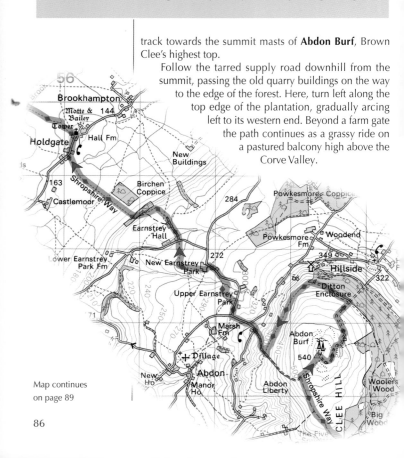

Map continues
on page 89

*Descending Brown Clee Hill towards the Corve Valley*

The path is clear for most of this section but beyond a gate at SO 588 869 it fades. However, the raised earthworks of an old wall above and left run parallel to the correct line and take it to a delightful sunken bridleway track, which descends the hillside of Abdon Liberty to a country lane.

On reaching the lane turn right down to a junction, where you turn left along a lane signed 'Abdon Village Hall', then right, on one signed 'Earnstrey'. After 200 metres go over a step-stile on the left and follow the hedge on the left, round the side and back of a sloping field. Cross two footbridges over streamlets and, over another stile by a gate, climb on a grass and dirt track back to a lane. Turn left along the lane.

As you come to **New Earnstrey Farm** there is a decision to be made. The Shropshire Way turns left just before the road corner and farm. It rounds the farm complex to the left before heading west with a hedge to the right across a couple of horribly cow-pocked fields. There is a

Even in dry weather the path around New Earnstrey Farm is ankle-twisting and awkward: the recommended route is to stay on the road and turn left at the next junction to return to the 'Way'.

crossing of a track that turns to slurry after wet periods. The path heads north over a stile on the right in the third field, heading north back to a lane opposite to the track leading to Earnstrey Hall. ◄

Follow the stony, grass-islanded track to **Earnstrey Hall**. This degenerates into a grassy, hedge-lined track beyond the houses. Where the track turns left, go straight on through a gate, then over a stile into fields. A square-towered church appears in the distance; you'll pass that later on. Follow the hedge as it curves gently left.

As the 'Way' approaches the woods of Mittons Rough, go left through a gate and angle across the small enclosure to the top of the woods. Watch out for the step-stile, which accesses a narrow winding path down through the woods. Beyond the stile at the bottom, the path descends gently northwest across fields parallel to **Birchen Coppice** on the right. There's a hedge on the left to act as a guide halfway down. On drawing level to Blue Hall (a small cottage) the path switches to the other side of the hedge but maintains direction. Over a stile and footbridge, it becomes enclosed for a short way and in the next field it veers right a little to round a field corner before aiming for the barns of Holdgate Farm. The path rounds these on the right to come out on the road at **Holdgate**.

> **Holdgate** today is a scattering of farms and cottages built on a low hill, but in medieval times up until the early 19th century it was larger and more important. It was founded and named after the Norman baron Helgot de Reisolent in 1086, who built a motte and bailey castle – the remains lie enshrouded by trees behind Hall Farm. Earthwork remains of the old village lie in fields to the south. The Holy Trinity church is mentioned in the Domesday Book but the current building dates back to the 12th century with later additions.

Turn right along the road to Holy Trinity church, the one you saw from the hill. Turn left on the track preceding

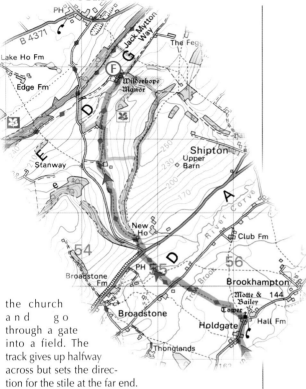

the church and go through a gate into a field. The track gives up halfway across but sets the direction for the stile at the far end.

The path now runs alongside a fence on the left, then over a stile by a gate and veers slightly left, still following a fence down to cross a footbridge over a dyke. The path maintains direction to a country lane. Go straight across, through a gate and turn immediately left by the hedge. At the first corner turn right, still following the field-edge, down to a concrete bridge, then climb to the busy B4378 Much Wenlock to Craven Arms road.

Turn right along the B-road for 20 metres, then left up the narrow lane signed 'Longville' and 'the Wilderhope Youth Hostel'. Beyond the first bend go over the step-stile

*The 16th-century Wilderhope Manor*

The 16th-century gabled mansion, now used as a youth hostel, is a Grade I Listed Building in the care of the National Trust.

on the right and angle across the field towards a stony track, which takes the route across the bridge and towards a cottage. Turn left across fields below the cottage, taking a course parallel to a tree-lined stream on the left.

On the approach to Lower Stanway Farm go left over a stile and footbridge, then over another stile to resume along the other side of the brook. Turn right along the farm drive encountered, then left at a signed gate. The path traces the left edge of a narrow field with a stream on the left at first. After crossing the stream the route continues north across fields and keeps the woods near the Bog to the left before joining a track, which leads you to **Wilderhope Manor.** ◄

90

# STAGE 8
## *Wilderhope to Ironbridge*

| | |
|---|---|
| **Start** | Wilderhope Manor YH |
| **Finish** | The Square, Ironbridge |
| **Distance** | 12½ miles (20.1km) |
| **Ascent** | 390m |
| **Descent** | 555m |
| **Time** | 6hr |
| **Terrain** | Woodland, ridge and field paths, country lanes |
| **Map** | OS Explorer 217 and 242 |
| **Supplies** | Much Wenlock |

From Wilderhope to Much Wenlock the Shropshire Way discovers Wenlock Edge, a 19-mile/31km wooded limestone escarpment formed over 400 million years ago when Shropshire was under the sea just south of the equator. Views to the left are often restricted by the trees and only give tantalising glimpses towards the Stretton Hills, but to the right you can look back across pastoral Corvedale to Brown Clee Hill. Much Wenlock is a wonderful and historic country town with a priory that is well worth visiting before resuming the journey to Ironbridge and the Severn Gorge, birthplace of the Industrial Revolution.

From the back of **Wilderhope Manor** car park climb the steps, continue through the gate and follow the way-marked route across fields to the rim of Wenlock Edge. Go through the gate on your right and take the inner (left fork) path through the top line of trees at first, then along the field edges.

The path comes to the corner of a narrow country lane. Here double back left to descend a signed path into the woods. Take the sharp right path and go straight ahead at the next junction. This leads to the B4371. Take the path immediately across the road, then the left fork, which leads down to the old Much Wenlock to Craven Arms railway

Map continues
on page 94

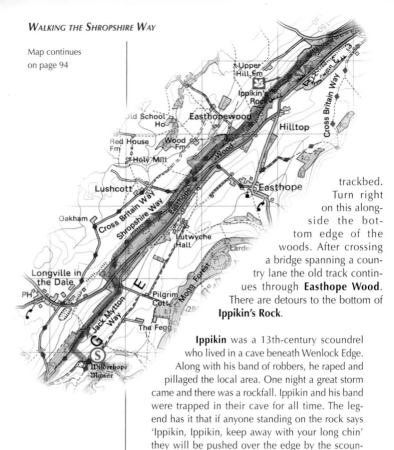

trackbed. Turn right on this alongside the bottom edge of the woods. After crossing a bridge spanning a country lane the old track continues through **Easthope Wood**. There are detours to the bottom of **Ippikin's Rock**.

**Ippikin** was a 13th-century scoundrel who lived in a cave beneath Wenlock Edge. Along with his band of robbers, he raped and pillaged the local area. One night a great storm came and there was a rockfall. Ippikin and his band were trapped in their cave for all time. The legend has it that if anyone standing on the rock says 'Ippikin, Ippikin, keep away with your long chin' they will be pushed over the edge by the scoundrel's ghost.

Stay with the main track, ignoring all rising paths to the right until you come to a signed Shropshire Way path on the left (SO 576 972). The path descends to the road. Turn right uphill along the road then turn left at the road junction. Just beyond this, turn left through a car park before taking the nearest path on the right. This undulating path passes an old limestone quarry and a bird hide before veering left, then right to follow a path with the huge Lea Quarry on the right. The old quarry is used by various factories including a woodyard.

On the way you'll come across a couple of viewpoints. The first encountered is **Major's Leap**.

## MAJOR'S LEAP

*Major's Leap, Wenlock Edge*

The major referred to is Major Thomas Smallman, a Royalist officer from Wilderhope Manor. He was carrying important dispatches when he was intercepted by Cromwellian forces. After a frantic chase he found himself cornered hereabouts on Wenlock Edge. Rather than surrender he rode his horse over the edge – a leap of over 60m. The horse was instantly killed but the major's fall was halted by an apple tree. He successfully delivered the dispatches on foot to Shrewsbury.

There is a good view of the Stretton Hills. Caer Caradoc with its rock-ruffled crest is the most prominent. Behind it is the sprawling Long Mynd ridge. In spring the view may be coloured by the vivid yellows of oil-seed rape. The path at this time will be decorated by wild violas, wood anemones, primroses, bluebells and wild garlic.

Further along the path you'll also see a short, signed diversion to the Wrekin viewpoint, where you can see the afforested whaleback beyond the plains of the Severn Valley.

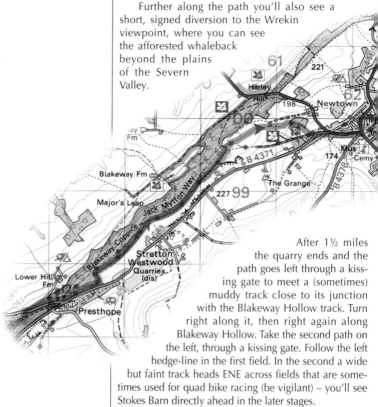

After 1½ miles the quarry ends and the path goes left through a kissing gate to meet a (sometimes) muddy track close to its junction with the Blakeway Hollow track. Turn right along it, then right again along Blakeway Hollow. Take the second path on the left, through a kissing gate. Follow the left hedge-line in the first field. In the second a wide but faint track heads ENE across fields that are sometimes used for quad bike racing (be vigilant) – you'll see Stokes Barn directly ahead in the later stages.

Join the track heading towards the barn. Where the track turns left in front of the barn go straight ahead through a gate, keeping to the left-hand side of a small field. Go through a kissing gate at the far end then turn right to enter a large field, with the grassed over quarry ahead and a zip wire to the left. The path descends into the quarry basin and passes beneath the zip wire – take care! At the far left end of the quarry the Way enters the woods via a wide farm gate. Take the path on the right,

which enters the woods before re-meeting the Blakeway Hollow track, now a tarred lane near to its exit with the Church Stretton B-road.

Map continues on page 96

Turn left along the road, past houses to join the A458, where you should turn right, following the pavement into **Much Wenlock** and onto High Street by the Gaskell Arms Hotel. This leads past the shops and inns to the Square in the centre of the small town.

## MUCH WENLOCK

The small market town grew alongside the monastery founded here in AD680 by Saxon King Merewalh of Mercia. In the early 12th century the monastery was refounded by the Normans for Cluniac monks. At this time the bones of St Milburga, the daughter of King Merewalh, were found and the news attracted pilgrims from far and wide. Although it was destroyed in the Dissolution of the Monasteries, there are still substantial ruins of the elaborate St Milburga's Priory.

These days the Holy Trinity parish church on the Green and the Guildhall dominate the centre of the town. The Cluniac monks built the church and the nave for that period is still intact. The square crenelated tower once had a spire but that was dismantled in the 1930s. The ground floor of the 16th-century half-timbered Guildhall was once a corn market but is now used for market stalls. On the first floor there's a courtroom, active until 1985, and current council chamber.

One of the twin mascots for the 2012 Olympic Games in London was called Wenlock and it's no coincidence, for in 1850 local surgeon Dr William Penny Brooks established the Wenlock Olympian Games. These started in the town before being held all around Shropshire. Brookes then set up the National Olympian Association, which had its first Games in 1866 at the Crystal Palace in London, an event that attracted 10,000 visitors and acted as one of the catalysts for the modern Olympic Games.

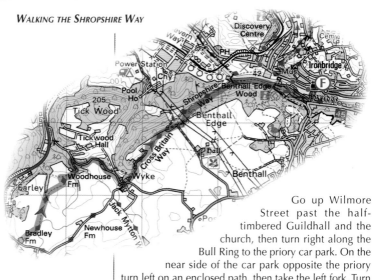

Go up Wilmore Street past the half-timbered Guildhall and the church, then turn right along the Bull Ring to the priory car park. On the near side of the car park opposite the priory turn left on an enclosed path, then take the left fork. Turn right on Station Road to pass the Old Station House before continuing ahead on a path bordering Linden Fields. Go right on a dirt path onto the old railway trackbed, where you should turn left, but after 360 metres leave it for a stepped path on the right next to an information board. This leads to a lane by the town's sewage works.

Follow the eastbound lane past the sewage works, then turn left to Downs Mill. Keep to the right of the mill and its pretty surrounding cottages to cross a wooden footbridge over a dyke, then head northeast across a field (a Shropshire Way sign highlights the direction). Keep to the hedge-line on the left edge of the next field before continuing on a hedge-lined track leading to the brick buildings (some derelict) of **Bradley Farm**.

After taking the track round to the right side of the farmyard go through a kissing gate at the back and head northeast across a large field before turning left alongside a hedge across two fields. At a waymarking post go right down some steps and over a culverted stream (SO 637 020). Head ENE towards a large tree slightly to the left of the brow of the hill. On reaching this turn left, then right along the nearside of the far hedge. Go through a kissing gate onto a track, which passes **Woodhouse Farm**. Follow the track through the woodland of Acklands Coppice out to a country lane.

Turn right along the lane to reach the hamlet of **Wyke**. After taking the left fork lane leave it at a sharp right-hand bend by Vineyards Farm for a stony track. This leads to a cluster of cottages marked as the Vineyards on current maps.

Go through a kissing gate behind the houses and climb to a stile in the top left-hand corner of the field. Now follow the hedge to another stile, which leads into **Benthall Edge Wood**. A path runs along the high edge of the wood. Ignore the left fork path descending towards Buildwas but stay high for now.

The Benthall Hall bridleway soon comes in from the right and the woodland path goes straight ahead through a gate. The path undulates and passes former limestone quarry pits, now leafy hollows. ▶

Beyond this the path divides. Take the lower left fork, which angles down towards the River Severn. At the time

The limestone geology allows the proliferation of rare species, including butterfly and bee orchids.

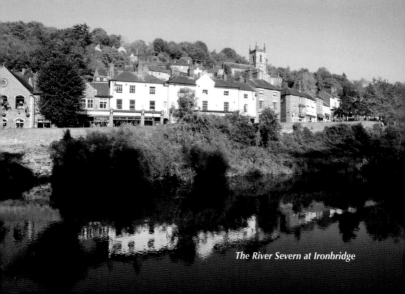

*The River Severn at Ironbridge*

of writing the cooling towers of the old Ironbridge coal-fired power station were still standing but after considerable debate they are about to be demolished.

On reaching a kissing gate turn right along a path that descends to the old railway trackbed of the Severn Valley line, which ran from Shrewsbury to Kidderminster. A short way on, at Bower Yard, are the remains of an old siding and lime kilns.

Continue along the old railway to a road, where a left turn takes you over the famous old dusky red-painted Iron Bridge to the Square in the centre of **Ironbridge**.

## THE IRONBRIDGE GORGE

Lying deep in a wooded gorge gouged out by the River Severn, Ironbridge has become synonymous with the Industrial Revolution, a fact recognised by its achievement of becoming a UNESCO World Heritage Site. In 1708 Abraham Darby leased the Coalbrookdale furnace and started iron-smelting with coke. His plant would become the world's first mass producer of cast iron.

*The China Works at Coalport*

Thomas Pritchard designed the world's first cast iron bridge for Abraham Darby III in 1779 to link the important industrial towns of Broseley and Madeley. The towns would become known throughout the world for the production of tiles, clay pipes and bricks. John Wilkinson, a precision engineer of Broseley, built cylinders for early steam engines and also produced the first iron boat.

# STAGE 9
## Ironbridge to Wellington

| | |
|---|---|
| **Start** | The Square, Ironbridge |
| **Finish** | Market Square, Wellington |
| **Distance** | 11 miles (17.6km) |
| **Ascent** | 705m |
| **Descent** | 655m |
| **Time** | 6hr |
| **Terrain** | Woodland, ridge and field paths, country lanes, town streets |
| **Map** | OS Explorer 242 |
| **Supplies** | Ironbridge, Wellington |

The early part of the day is a fascinating mix of woodland and industrial archaeology as the route dips into Coalbrookdale and follows the Rope Walk up onto a high pastured plateau to remote Little Wenlock. Highlight of the day has to be the iconic Wrekin. The climb through woodland to the summit is steep but the craggy perches on top reward you with views across several counties. Finally, paths over the smaller, thickly wooded Ercall lead to Wellington.

From the Square in **Ironbridge** go east along High Street to a roundabout. Here turn back left up Church Hill, which you follow uphill for some 600 metres. At the end of the road turn right along Lincoln Hill, then left down the drive of Limeburners. A footpath sign directs the route to the right, off the drive and through the woods of Lincoln Hill.

Turn left at a crossing of paths along the one signed to the Rotunda. ▶ Follow the path left along the top of the woods to a clearing and an information board, the site of the Rotunda.

If you are short of time go straight ahead at all junctions, following signs down to Paradise (a road at the bottom of the woods).

The **Rotunda**, built in the 1790s by iron master Richard Reynolds, would have been a round, bandstand-like structure with cast iron pillars and a lead roof. Views would have been wide encompassing the village below, the Severn and the iron bridge. Today, although you can still see some of the bridge, trees obscure much of the lower town.

Descend from the Rotunda, soon using steps. Keep right, ignoring Ironbridge paths on the left. The route passes above some cottages before climbing gradually to a path intersection. Angle left down steps on the 'Paradise' path. This comes down to a rough lane where you turn left down to the road. Turn right along the road, passing below the youth hostel and out to the main road in **Coalbrookdale**.

Turn right along the main road, then fork left opposite a distinctive red-bricked chapel up on the right, onto the road down to the Museum of Iron – you'll see the clocktower on its roof. Turn left with the road, go under the railway viaduct and turn right along Darby Road, which soon veers left uphill.

Just beyond Tea Kettle Row fork right through gates along a track known as the Rope Walk. ◀ The track

The Rope Walk track follows the course of an old tramway where horses would pull small tubs of sandstone from Lydebrook Dingle to Coalbrookdale.

*Museum of Iron, Coalbrookdale*

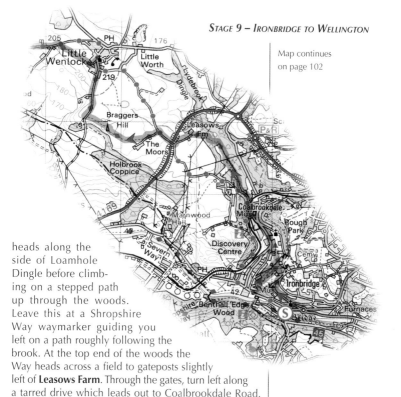

Map continues
on page 102

heads along the side of Loamhole Dingle before climbing on a stepped path up through the woods. Leave this at a Shropshire Way waymarker guiding you left on a path roughly following the brook. At the top end of the woods the Way heads across a field to gateposts slightly left of **Leasows Farm**. Through the gates, turn left along a tarred drive which leads out to Coalbrookdale Road. Turn right along this, crossing the bridge over the busy A4169 highway.

After nearly 300 metres turn left along a farm lane, passing Moors Cottage before going over a stile on the right by a double gate and angling westwards towards the first large tree in the fence to the left of this large field. Now follow the field boundary towards the masts on **Braggers Hill**. Go over a stile by a gate in the fence beneath the masts and turn immediately right then left on a rutted track leading to the Buildwas Lane. Turn right here to reach **Little Wenlock** village. ▸

At the road junction turn left to the square-towered church. The Way now leaves the village on Witchwell

By the first houses a view indicator highlights the wildly meandering River Severn and the hills across the southern horizon including Wenlock Edge, Caer Caradoc, the Long Mynd and Stiperstones.

101

Lane to the left. This soon curves right before becoming an enclosed path that, beyond two gates in a small enclosure, leads out to fields. Follow the right edge of the field to the next gate, where a tractor track with a hedge to the right leads out to a country lane. Turn left along the lane, take the next right fork, then follow it for about 1½ miles to the foot of the plantations cloaking the Wrekin.

Take the second footpath on the right and climb on a steep path through the woods with only a brief respite on the clearing of **Little Hill**. Ignore all forest tracks to the left and right on this section. As height is gained views improve and soon you come to the rocks known as the **Needle's Eye**, where you can see back past Little Wenlock to the Ironbridge Gorge.

Just beyond the rocks the path rises between the southwestern walls of the fort to the summit of **the Wrekin**. The summit is crowned by a trig point and a view indicator, which will tell you that the distinctive

Map continues on page 105

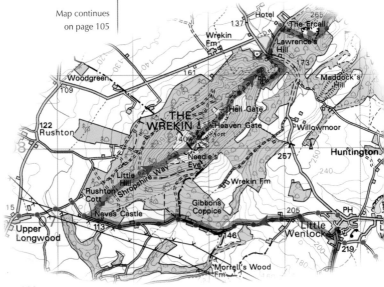

## THE WREKIN

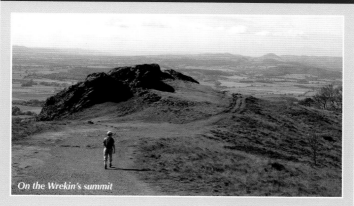

*On the Wrekin's summit*

Formed by volcanic eruptions triggered by the nearby Church Stretton fault, the Wrekin consists of various igneous rocks, including rhyolite and tuffs. There is a more romantic story of the mountain's origin involving a Welsh giant, Gwendol Wrekin ap Shenkin ap Mynyddmawr, who had a grudge against Shrewsbury. It was his intention to carry a great sack of earth and dam the River Severn, thus flooding the city and drowning its inhabitants. But he lost his way and somehow ended up near Wellington. The rapidly tiring giant encountered a cobbler who was coming from Shrewsbury carrying a sack full of shoes for repair. The giant told him of his plans. The quick-thinking cobbler told him that it was too far and a bad idea. He showed the giant his bag of shoes saying that he had worn out every single pair on the arduous journey. The giant, now too tired to proceed, dropped the mound of earth where he stood and scraped his shoes. The mound became the Wrekin and the scrapings, the Ercall.

The Wrekin's summit is capped by a large 20ha Iron Age fort, once home to the Cornovii tribe. The Romans built their city, Wroxeter, just 4 miles away and battles ensued with the Celtic leader, Virico. The Romans were victorious but Virico must have put up a good fight for the Romans named their city Viroconium in honour of their enemy. When the Normans came they renamed the hill Mount Gilbert but several centuries later the name reverted to being called the Wrekin.

looking hills to the southwest are Caer Caradoc, the seat of another ancient fort, and the Long Mynd.

A wide track now leads north-eastwards along the ridge, past a TV mast, then through inner and outer walls of the fort known as Heaven and Hell Gates respectively. Soon back in the forest, the track eventually does a U turn and comes to the Halfway House (café) marked on maps as Wrekin Cottage.

Beyond the cottage the track descends further then bends left, then left again to come to a road close to a junction and car park. Turn right for a short way, then left along the road signed to Wellington. After about 450 metres and by another car park, turn right on a Shropshire Way waymarked track that climbs ESE through woodland, past the disused Ercall Quarries before climbing left along the east shoulder of the hill. After being joined by a path from the summit the path eases slightly right then

*Old quarry on the Ercall*

over a footbridge spanning a brook before coming out onto Golf Links Road.

Go left along the road, under the motorway bridge. At a T-junction with the B5061 use the pedestrian crossing to the far side. The narrow enclosed onward path is staggered to the left and continues north passing some allotments before coming to another road. Cross this and take the footpath angling half-right between buildings. Turn left on meeting a road (Tan Bank). This comes to an end for traffic at a main road (Victoria Avenue). After crossing the road take the road opposite (still Tan Bank). Where the road swings right, go left into a pedestrian area leading to Market Square in the centre of **Wellington**.

## WELLINGTON

Wellington is the largest of Telford's borough towns and its population, when separated from Telford, would make it Shropshire's third largest. Its name is derived from Weola, an Anglo Saxon farmer who worked the lands hereabouts. We do know that Roman soldiers marched here for they built their road, Watling Street, traversing what is now the southern part of the town to link London with Viroconium (Wroxeter).

The town was known as Wellington under the Wrekin during medieval times and was granted a market charter in 1244. The original church was mentioned in the Domesday Book but was damaged in the Civil War and eventually replaced by the current All Saints Church in 1790 to a grand design by George Steuart, the architect who designed the Attingham Park mansion between Wellington and Shrewsbury.

# STAGE 10
*Wellington to Haughmond*

| | |
|---|---|
| **Start** | Market Square, Wellington |
| **Finish** | Haughmond Abbey entrance |
| **Distance** | 11¾ miles (19km) |
| **Ascent** | 150m |
| **Descent** | 150m |
| **Time** | 6hr |
| **Terrain** | Forest, park and field paths, country lanes, town streets |
| **Map** | OS Explorer 242 |
| **Supplies** | Wellington |
| **Transport** | 519 Arriva service to Shrewsbury (from Newport) stops at Haughmond Abbey |
| **Accommodation** | Although there are campsites there is no other accommodation near the abbey. The Haughmond (hotel) in Upton Magna just before the hill is a possible alternative. |

This is an easy section, with just one low hill, that of Haughmond. The way out through the Wellington suburbs is surprisingly pleasant, with good paths taking the route around the nature reserve of Dothill Park, where there are woods and a number of lakes. Most of the farmland west of Admaston is prairie-like and used for arable crops. Poppies in the wheat may well remind you of Van Gogh paintings. Haughmond at day's end is a delightful place with fine views through its trees to Shrewsbury's spires and the hills of west Shropshire, with the Welsh borders fading into the horizon.

Leave **Wellington** from the clock in the square and head north up Church Street, over the railway bridge and past All Saints Church. Turn left along Vineyard Road. Beyond Vineyard Drive use the stony path running parallel to the road. Turn right along North Road passing the schools before turning left on Deer Park Road. Just beyond the bend in the road, turn off left across open ground in

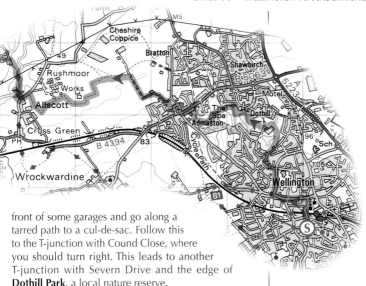

front of some garages and go along a
tarred path to a cul-de-sac. Follow this
to the T-junction with Cound Close, where
you should turn right. This leads to another
T-junction with Severn Drive and the edge of
**Dothill Park**, a local nature reserve.

Map continues
on page 109

Follow the tarred footpath/cycleway ahead through
the park, past a tree-enshrouded lake and go straight on
past the schools, which should be kept to the left. Take the
left turn at the junction then fork right just short of a road
(Seven Drive). The tarred path continues on the other side
of the road and rounds a tree-lined lake, known as Tee
Lake on account of its shape (but not named on current
OS maps). Just beyond the northwest corner of the lake,
fork right to head north by a couple of narrow sheets of
water. Beyond the second the path swings left, crosses
a footbridge and takes a winding course to join an old
railway track-bed, which it follows north. Just before a
concrete bridge fork right on a tarred path to a road at
**Admaston**.

Turn left over the bridge and along the road, past the
Pheasant (inn), then right at Bratton Road which becomes
Elmsdale Cresent beyond a chapel. Follow the road left,
around to the second bend where the route continues
along a fenced path beginning between two drives. This

107

The line of the right of way marked on current OS maps follows the hedge-line to the left: this may be impassable due to thick vegetation.

St George's Church in Rodington is mentioned in the Domesday Book, although it was much modified in the 19th century.

*River Tern at Alscott*

turns right before coming to a lane. Turn left here and follow it past Cheshire Coppice Cottages. The lane traverses prairie-like crop fields. After 700 metres turn left off the road onto a waymarked field path with a hedge on the left. The route switches sides of the hedge at SJ 623 135. Follow the field margins on the right, on a path that goes left, right and left again before turning right to follow a grassy track across an uncultivated weed-strewn field. ◄

The track brings the route to a hedge-lined grass track passing to the left of a sewage works. Turn right through a waymarked gate before following the line of the hedge on the left across fields to the lane at **Allscott**.

Turn left along the lane. After 170 metres turn right to follow the drive of Allscott Mill (B&B). Pass to the right of the house and cross the footbridge over the delightful River Tern. After following the riverbank for 500 metres turn left to **Isombridge Farm** to reach a lane corner. Go straight ahead along the lane, take the right fork after 250 metres, then a left at the next junction and follow the lane into **Rodington**. ◄

Just past the church, turn left. Then, beyond the houses, turn right to head west across fields. The path

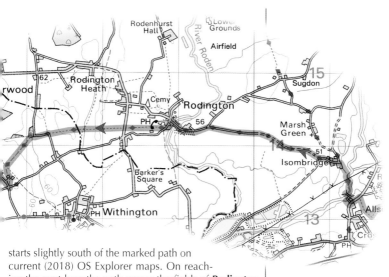

starts slightly south of the marked path on current (2018) OS Explorer maps. On reaching the next lane the path across the fields of **Rodington Heath** is staggered slightly to the left. The Wrekin is very dominant to the south across cereal fields.

Map continues on page 110

The path passes a tree-lined pond, then a plank bridge at the far end of the huge field. It continues across a stile and through a gap to reach another lane near a corner. Turn right along the lane which, almost immediately, bends left. At the next corner leave the lane for a path through a farm gate on the left. This goes alongside some trees on the left then goes left to cross a footbridge before heading southwest towards the buildings of **Hunkington Farm**.

There are electric fences around horse paddocks on both sides. After 40 metres turn half-left through a bridlegate and follow the clear bridleway out through four further gates to a lane. Turn right to pass in front of the farm.

Follow the waymarked bridleway on the far side of the lane. This heads WSW across a large field towards a wood. The path then traces the left edge of the wood to reach a farm cross-track at the far end. Turn right here,

The pleasant village of Upton Magna lies just to the south, with a pub/hotel, the Haughmond, and a village shop with a nice café.

then take the second gap on the left, and head southwest alongside a hedge and with a small reservoir on the left – it's the opposite side to that shown on the 2018 Explorer maps. The path follows the hedge on the left to a lane, where the Shropshire Way turns right. ◄

After 700 metres leave the lane for a stony forestry track on the left at Criftin Gate. This soon turns right, uphill. Stay with the main track as it bends left beyond a covered reservoir but take the next Shropshire Way signed right turn at SJ 548 137. The path passes beneath broad-leaved trees. After 600 metres make a left turn to head SSW. After 500 metres this reaches another junction. Take the path veering slightly right (northwest). After 300 metres at SJ 538 138 the Way turns right.

A short **there-and-back detour** on the track ahead should be taken to the area marked fort on the map before taking this right turn. Large display slabs show the local rocks and there's also a view indicator. To the west you look across the fields of Uffington to Shrewsbury and its spires, across the plains of the

River Severn to the distinctive Breidden Hills and further beyond to the hills of Mid Wales. Looking south the distinctive slightly serrated top of Caer Caradoc leads the eye to the Long Mynd ridge and the Stiperstones.

Back on the main waymarked path, you wind through the forest and along the quarry borders. A signed detour left halfway along this stretch leads to the quarry rim viewpoint, where you can study the rock strata on the quarry face. Eventually the path comes to the car park behind the café and picnic area. The café serves sandwiches, cakes and drinks.

Follow the tarred drive out to the road. Turn left along the road, passing the entrance to the quarry before reaching the B-road. Turn left again. The onward path passing to the west of **Haughmond Abbey** is on the right after 250 metres. ▶

*Shrewsbury from Haughmond Hill*

If you've booked accommodation in Shrewsbury the 519 Newport to Shrewsbury bus stops a few paces beyond.

111

# STAGE 10A
*Haughmond to Shrewsbury link*

| | |
|---|---|
| **Start** | Haughmond Abbey entrance |
| **Finish** | Kingsland Bridge, Shrewsbury |
| **Distance** | 5¼ miles (8.3km) |
| **Ascent** | 45m |
| **Descent** | 90m |
| **Time** | 2½hr |
| **Terrain** | Woodland, riverside and field paths, unsurfaced lanes, canal towpath |
| **Map** | OS Explorer 241 |

Section 10A has been included for the benefit of those wanting to complete the southern circular but omit the northern one. It also allows for a northern circular based on Shrewsbury, and so the route has been described in both directions. It is a short and very pleasant hike following forestry paths, a canal that has returned to nature and the delightful banks of the Severn.

From the entrance of **Haughmond Abbey** go back down the drive to cross the B5062 road, turn left along it then turn right on the path signed 'the Hollies'. This passes through pleasant woodland to the west of the Haughmond Stone Quarry, which is hidden from here. After 1200 metres take the right fork path. Just beyond the point the path passes under electricity pylons turn left out of the forest, across a field and over Brickkiln Bridge, which spans the old Shrewsbury Canal, water-filled hereabouts.

The **Shrewsbury Canal**, engineered by Thomas Telford, opened in 1797 linking Shrewsbury and Trench, where it served the coal mines and iron-works of the area. Telford's aqueduct at Longdon on Tern was the first constructed of iron and was the forerunner of the famous one at Pontycysyllte near Chirk. In the early days the narrow canal took trains of horse-drawn tubs but in 1835 the Newport Canal was opened and joined the Shrewsbury Canal to the national network. At this time the Shrewsbury Canal was widened to take narrowboats.

As with most canals the coming of the railways curtailed activities and the Shrewsbury Canal fared badly, with most of the infrastructure disappearing in the 20th century. However, the Shrewsbury and Newport Canals Trust has embarked upon ambitious plans to restore the section from the Buttermarket in Shrewsbury to the Shropshire Union Canal at Norbury Junction.

Continue along a grass track towards the houses of **Uffington**, then along a tarred lane, which meets the

*By the old Shrewsbury Canal at Heathgates*

main road opposite the Corbet Arms. Turn right here and follow the road past the Holy Trinity Church before turning left along Mill Lane. This descends briefly towards the River Severn, and passes in front of a mansion. Continue along a path through a short stretch of trees beyond the mansion, then alongside a field

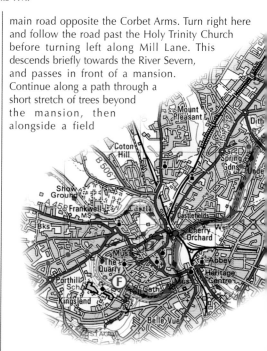

edge. Beyond a gate turn left on a grass track on an embankment that was part of the Shrewsbury Canal. Follow this under the bridge carrying the A49. The path crosses a tarred lane north of **Pimley Manor** and follows the line of the old canal: an information sign here shows you are now entering the Old Shrewsbury Canal Countryside Site.

At a four-way meeting of tracks, highlighted by blue cycle route signs, turn left, following the Shropshire Way and descending to the banks of the Severn. Turn right on a narrow riverside path, which passes under the A5112 bridge before joining a quiet lane (Sydney Avenue) in Castle Fields. The lane, used mainly by walkers, anglers and cyclists, leads the route to a weir. ◄

Occasionally the river floods this next riverside section in which case you'll have to divert right along parallel roads.

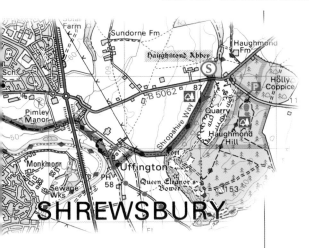

Beyond the weir follow a surfaced riverside track to the railway bridge. If you're catching a train climb the steps just before the huge railway bridge and turn left just beyond Shrewsbury Jail (now closed) on a footbridge to the station. Otherwise, continue by the river, under the English Bridge to the Kingsland Bridge in the centre of **Shrewsbury**.

*The Severn on the outskirts of Shrewsbury*

**Reverse direction: Shrewsbury to Haughmond**

From the Kingsland Bridge follow the tarred path along the north bank of the Severn, passing under the English Bridge, where you'll be able to see the sandstone tower of Shrewsbury Abbey. Continue along the path beneath the railway station. Beyond an impressive weir the route joins Sydney Avenue. As that curves away to the left the Way continues by the river on a narrow tree-lined path that soon passes under the A5112. The path leaves the river and climbs to a four-way cycleway junction. Turn right here on what was the towpath of the old Shrewsbury Canal, water-filled hereabouts.

The canal soon becomes dry but a track continues and crosses a tarred lane north of **Pimley Manor** then under the bridge carrying the A49. Beyond this it curves gently to the right, still following the course of the canal. The Shropshire Way leaves the track for a field path on the right. This eventually passes through some trees and in front of a grand house overlooking the Severn. Continue on the lane ahead, which comes out at the main road in **Uffington**.

Turn right, passing the Holy Trinity Church, then left on the tarred lane of Tower Farm opposite the Corbet Arms. At the end maintain direction along a field edge and go over the Brickkiln Bridge, which spans the old Shrewsbury Canal, now water-filled again. After crossing another field, the path enters a narrow woodland strip, where it turns right. Take the next left fork path and head north through more woodland (the Hollies) to the west of the hidden Haughmond Stone Quarry. The path comes out on the busy B5062 road. Turn left then right along the drive of **Haughmond Abbey**. You have now joined the main Shropshire Way route to the north of the county.

# STAGE 11
## Haughmond to Wem

| | |
|---|---|
| **Start** | Haughmond Abbey entrance |
| **Finish** | St Peter and Paul's Church, Wem |
| **Distance** | 11¾ miles (18.9km) |
| **Ascent** | 160m |
| **Descent** | 170m |
| **Time** | 6hr |
| **Terrain** | Field paths, country lanes |
| **Map** | OS Explorer 241 |
| **Supplies** | Hadnall, Wem |

Today the Shropshire Way starts its journey around north Shropshire; across very rural landscapes, where flatlands are punctuated by small sandstone hills. One of the highlights of the day, the expansive ruins of Haughmond Abbey, comes straight away, followed by the woods and the sandstone cliffs of Grinshill. By detouring to explore the latter you'll get to see fine views of the surrounding countryside and the great sandstone rocks that helped with the building of Shrewsbury. The day ends in Wem, a quiet country town so typical of north Shropshire.

Just short of the entrance to **Haughmond Abbey** go through a kissing gate on the left and trace the west and north perimeters of the grounds. The path enters a narrow strip of woodland, crosses a woodland track and comes to a large field opposite Haughmond Farm. Angle half-right here and go through a roadside gate before turning left to follow the drive towards **Haughmond Farm**. Keep to the left of the buildings before heading northwards on an ever-so-straight green lane. This ends on the southwest side of **Ebury Hill**. ▸

The fort is obscured by a campsite and thick woods.

Turn left here and follow a fence on the left, south-westwards back to New Coppice. The path turns right,

## HAUGHMOND ABBEY

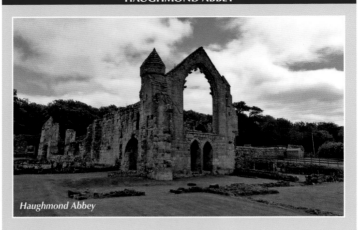

*Haughmond Abbey*

Although the origins are disputed, the probability is that a hermitage and a chapel were established at Haughmond in the early 12th century. By 1155 it had become an Augustinian abbey dedicated to St John the Evangelist and under the patronage of William FitzAlan.

The abbey became very prosperous with grants coming in from very influential people, including Henry II. Unfortunately, it was also synonymous with abuse of power and corruption. Although the dozen or so canons and priests lived in penury, the Abbots lived in style in a palatial lodging house.

Haughmond became the FitzAlan shrine, with all heads of the family after William buried there for over 150 years. The abbey was destroyed during Henry VIII's Dissolution in 1539. The ruins are still impressive and are in the custodianship of English Heritage.

following the edge of the woods, then right again, heading towards the northeast corner and the distant red-bricked Haughmond Villa. At the far end of the field go through a gate and follow the hedge on the left as it arcs gently leftwards. The bridleway soon becomes a farm track leading to the **Wheatley complex**. On the final approaches look out for a gate on the right. Beyond this follow a stony track to the north, which soon becomes a winding grass track that ends a short way after a right-hand bend. Here, go through a gate on the left and follow the line of the hedge on the right, out to the busy A53 road at **Upper Astley**.

After crossing and turning right along the road, turn left by the Dog in the Lane pub and follow the lane through the houses to the charming village of **Astley**, which is part of a conservation area due to its number of listed buildings.

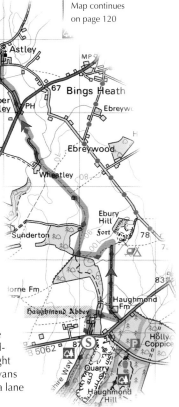

Map continues on page 120

**Astley**, which was mentioned in the Domesday Book, was once administered by Haughmond Abbey. The square-towered St Mary's, Church, which dates back to the 12th century, has a 13th-century bell – it's very rare for such bells to survive so long. The whitewashed Corinthian-style mansion of Astley House, which you will see across fields on the approach to the village, is a much-enlarged development of an 18th-century house.

The lane turns left by the church, then right, but on the apex of the second bend leave the lane for a stony track. Where the track divides leave it through a gate between the two branches, then follow the hedge keeping to the left of a shed before going through a kissing gate onto an enclosed path. At the end of this follow a hedge on the right before angling right across the field-corner, keeping the caravans and lodges of Beaconsfield to the left. Cross a lane

119

Map continues
on page 123

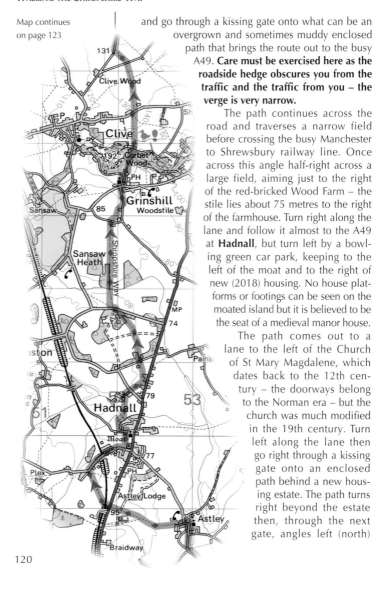

and go through a kissing gate onto what can be an overgrown and sometimes muddy enclosed path that brings the route out to the busy A49. **Care must be exercised here as the roadside hedge obscures you from the traffic and the traffic from you – the verge is very narrow.**

The path continues across the road and traverses a narrow field before crossing the busy Manchester to Shrewsbury railway line. Once across this angle half-right across a large field, aiming just to the right of the red-bricked Wood Farm – the stile lies about 75 metres to the right of the farmhouse. Turn right along the lane and follow it almost to the A49 at **Hadnall**, but turn left by a bowling green car park, keeping to the left of the moat and to the right of new (2018) housing. No house platforms or footings can be seen on the moated island but it is believed to be the seat of a medieval manor house.

The path comes out to a lane to the left of the Church of St Mary Magdalene, which dates back to the 12th century – the doorways belong to the Norman era – but the church was much modified in the 19th century. Turn left along the lane then go right through a kissing gate onto an enclosed path behind a new housing estate. The path turns right beyond the estate then, through the next gate, angles left (north)

120

across a field with paddocks to the right. After passing to the right of an outbuilding the path goes through a kissing gate onto another path through some trees then onto Ladymas Lane, where the route turns right to a lane junction. Maintain direction across the lane by going through a gate and following the hedge on the left. The path nears the houses along the A49 but turns left behind their back-garden walls and fences. Through a gate it crosses fields, veering slightly right before straightening out and heading for a cottage in a hedged enclosure. Keep to the right of this enclosure to reach the unsurfaced Mill Lane.

Turn right along the lane then turn left on the nearside of a rustic sandstone cottage to pass along the edge of woodland before heading across fields. After crossing a track/horse gallop aim for a gate on the edge of the woodland surrounding Hardwicke Stables, now a rural industrial complex.

The distinguished soldier **Sir Rowland Hill** owned a large mansion, Hardwicke Grange, now the site of this complex. He was one of the Duke of Wellington's great generals in the Battle of Waterloo (1815) and became Commander-in-chief of the British Army in 1828. Lord Hill's Column in Shrewsbury is the tallest Doric column in England.

Through the gate, angle left across scrub overgrown with vegetation, including nettles. Keep the buildings to the left before coming to a lane. Turn left along this before turning right on a track heading north towards the woods of New Plantation. Cross another gallop, but don't follow it northwards but instead go through a gate and take the path along a grassy ride, parallel and to the left of it.

Go through a gate ahead as the track turns right and aim for another gate in the far right corner of the field. Follow the hedge on the right out to a lane. At the time of writing, the continuing path 20 metres to the right along the lane had been obscured at the hedge at SJ 520 230. This made the continuing stretch of path difficult. If this is still the case when you go it is best to turn right along the

*Looking back southwards from the summit of Grinshill*

## GRINSHILL STONE

Grinshill stone is a sandstone that has been quarried here since Roman times. Fossils from the Triassic period, including skeletons and footprints of the Rhynchosaurus, a primitive lizard-like reptile, have been discovered here. The site has been designated as a county wildlife site and a SSSI for its geological importance. Corbet Wood, which cloaks the hill, is a local nature reserve, for the mixed woodland provides a wonderful habitat for many birds, including woodpeckers, warblers and goldcrests. The area is known too for its many species of butterfly and moth.

The sandstone has been used in many of Shropshire's buildings such as Haughmond Abbey, many of the local churches, Shrewsbury's railway station and the Welsh Bridge. More famously, it can be seen on the door surrounds of 10 Downing Street and in the building at Chequers.

lane and turn left at the next junction to reach a T-junction below All Saints Church in the village of **Grinshill**.

To get the best views, which include the northern plains and the distant Shrewsbury, a detour to the trig point on the summit is necessary. A path begins at SJ 522 239.

Turn right, then left by the church to reach the village hall. Climb the path to the left of the hall into **Corbet Wood**. Where the main path divides (by an information board), take the left fork, which maintains its northerly direction and comes to a stony track by some cottages. Turn left along it for a few paces then turn right to pass to the left of one of them, crossing a lawned area before going through a gate onto fields. Follow the hedge on the right at first but pass through a gateway and follow its right side in the latter stages to reach a roadside kissing gate at Quarry View, just east of the village of Clive.

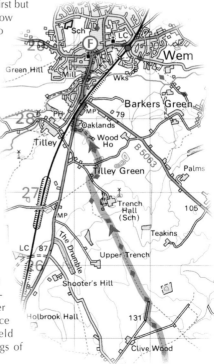

Turn right along the road then left through another kissing gate and follow the hedge on the right across two fields. Angle slightly left across the next, passing just to the left of a tree-lined pond before crossing a farm lane and continuing across fields, now with the hedge to the left. Pass to the left of another tree-lined pond to reach a hedge-enclosed grass track. Turn right along it but after 180 metres turn left through a kissing gate.

After cutting a corner across the next small field the path follows a hedge on the left. After switching sides of the hedge twice the path reaches an open field on the approach to the buildings of

123

**Trench Hall School** (the Woodlands Centre). Here, the Shropshire Way follows the line marked on the current Explorer maps with black dashes and not the green dashes of the right of way. This takes a course far nearer the school buildings.

> **Trench Hall** today is the Woodlands Centre, incorporating the Woodlands School. In the past, it provided a different educational function. In the 1930s Adolf Hitler denied Jewish people the right to become teachers or their children to be educated. In 1933 Anna Essinger decided she would flee the country with all of her pupils and set up a school in England. The first was in Bunce Hall, Kent, but after war broke out between the nations there was ill feeling and the school was relocated to the much smaller Trench Hall. Overcrowding made conditions difficult and in 1946 the pupils returned to Bunce Hall.

Beyond the old school, aim for a red-bricked house when it comes into view. On reaching the lane by the cottage, continue across it, following a grass track before angling left across a field. The path passes to the right of another laneside cottage. Cross the lane and go over a stile on the other side to pass between two lily pools before heading NNW across a large field towards the pretty whitewashed Pankeymoor Cottages. On reaching them follow the drive out to the lane at Oaklands.

Turn right along the busy B5476 Wem road. After passing the churchyard onto High Street, you reach the centre of **Wem**.

**WEM**

*The main street of Wem from the church grounds*

Although the Iron Age Cornovii tribe settled in these parts, the town of Wem dates back to Saxon times, when it was known as Wamm, meaning marsh, a reference to the marshy ground which then surrounded the River Roden. Today's travellers will see some nice Georgian buildings but will note that there are no really old buildings. The history of the town will show you why.

Firstly, they had a motte and bailey castle built by William Pantulf. You can see the mound behind the church. The castle was enlarged by Hugh Pantulf in the 13th century with the wooden structures being replaced by stone buildings. By the time of the Wars of the Roses there were town walls and a powerful castle but both town and castle were 'torn apart' by the Yorkists led by the Earl of Salisbury. In the Civil War the townsfolk, including many women, repelled the 5000 Royalists troops of Lord Capel. The battle is commemorated in song: "The Women of Wem and a few musketeers, beat Lord Capel and his Cavaliers." In 1677, Jane Churn, a 14-year-old, dropped a candle which started a fire that destroyed most of the town. Even the church bells melted under the intense heat and had to be recast.

Famous Wem residents include the 'Hanging' Judge Jeffreys from Low Hall and the essayist William Hazlitt, whose childhood home was in Noble Street.

# STAGE 12
## *Wem to Ellesmere*

| | |
|---|---|
| **Start** | St Peter and Paul's Church, Wem |
| **Finish** | High Street, Ellesmere |
| **Distance** | 14½ miles (23.4km) |
| **Ascent** | 120m |
| **Descent** | 105m |
| **Time** | 6hr |
| **Terrain** | Field paths, country lanes, canal towpath, town streets |
| **Map** | OS Explorer 241 |
| **Supplies** | Wem, Ellesmere |
| **Note** | In this stage, at Welsh End Corner, there is an option to divert from the main route to visit Whitchurch and Grindley Brook Locks, which links with the Sandstone Trail. This is covered in the next section, Stage 12A, which is written in both directions, enabling the town to be used as both a finishing point for those who want to cut short the route or for an alternative starting point for those who want to do the whole Way including the leg. |

The Ellesmere route is highlighted by glacial mosses and meres, fascinating places for flora and fauna. The route also joins the Llangollen branch of the Shropshire Union Canal, which offers a well-paced walk into Ellesmere.

Starting from St Peter and Paul's Church on the High Street in **Wem** head east past the town hall to the Castle Inn. Turn left along a little ginnel on the far side of the inn and follow it for around 400 metres. On reaching Pyms Road cross it and go up Wemsbrook Road, which is opposite and staggered slightly to the right. Turn right on Marlcroft, the third road on the right. Ignore the first left but follow the road around the left-hand bend, which soon comes to a cul-de-sac. Go through another ginnel ahead, highlighted by a Shropshire Way post, to reach

Barnfield Avenue, where you turn right for a few paces before continuing through a hedge-lined passageway which soon turns left into fields on the edge of town.

Map continues on page 131

A clear path, enclosed by hedges and a fence at first, heads north across the fields to a lane at **Ryebank**, along which the route turns right. At the T-junction the Way goes through a kissing gate staggered slightly to the left across the road and follows the hedge on the left at first. In the second field it aims for the left side of a tree-surrounded pond before angling left across the corner of a field. The orange Shropshire Way signs highlight the route across more stiles as the route heads north across a huge field, which often has crops in it. Aim slightly to the right of a large tree among some bushes and towards a distant white house. The trees turn out to be the surrounds of a large pond. Continue towards a white house to the left of which a track will lead out to the road opposite St Mary's Church on the edges of **Edstaston**.

**St Mary's Church** is a Grade I listed 12th-century church, built with local sandstone. It has been described as one of the most complete Romanesque buildings in Shropshire. The church's combined nave and chancel including the three doorways are all Norman, while the bellcote and vestry were added in the 19th century.

127

*St Mary's Church
at Edstaston*

After turning left along the lane past a coach depot and the remains of the old Prees branch of the Ellesmere Canal the route comes to a hairpin bend. Turn right off the lane here on a track that soon bends left and heads towards a lorry depot. Just before this watch out for a stile on the left by a recently built house (2018). This leads to a wide grass path that passes through trees before veering left to round the huge sheds of the Oaklands Egg factory.

The path veers right (north) by a tree-enclosed pond then, through a kissing gate, continues north across fields, passing another pond before joining a muddy track out to a country lane. After turning right along the lane, turn right at the next junction. Keep straight on at the next junction following the lane signed to Whixall and Bostock Hall.

The lane comes to a T-junction at **Whixall**. The short track wanted next is staggered to the left. It is sometimes choked with nettles and other vegetation. If this is the case turn right, then next left. At the bend by Church Farm go down the drive for a short way to reach the north end of the previously mentioned track. Go through the kissing gate directly ahead here (or to your left if you've braved the track) and head north across fields. After crossing a farm track, built from concrete sleepers the Way passes

## FENN'S WHIXALL AND BETTISFIELD NATURE RESERVE

The mosses are natural ombrotrophic raised peat bogs, which means their only source of water is the rainfall. The mosses were damaged in recent centuries by drainage for the canal and railways and by commercial cutting of peat, which began in 1851. At first tramways were built for horse-drawn wagons. In 1919 the horses were replaced by internal combustion-engined locomotives, then tractors. This all ended in 1990 when the Nature Conservancy Council bought the leases and endeavoured to restore the mosses by blocking the drains and digging up the scrub woodland.

The reserve is now home to many rare species of bog moss, including the rare Waved and Fork-mosses. You'll also see insect-eating sundew with their sticky red-tinged green leaves, bog rosemary, which have drooping pink and white blooms, the yellow-flowered bog asphodel and white-beaked sedge, which has small white flowers.

The remaining ditches of the mosses are inhabited by water voles, while adders can be seen on the drier spots. There are over 600 species of moth on the reserve and 32 species of butterfly, including the brimstone, the green hairstreak and the large heath, which thrives on the heathland and cotton sedge. The reserve is also home to many species of dragonfly and damselfly, including the white-faced darter dragonfly.

*Thriving Whixall Moss*

The path over the bridge ahead is the route to Whitchurch described in Stage 12A.

to the right of an enclosed pond before crossing another concrete track. It runs alongside one in the next field and passes left of another pond to meet an important junction of routes at **Welsh End Corner**. ◄

Go to the left following a hedge on the left to a country lane. Turn right along the lane, then take the next left fork signed to Whixall Moss. After passing a school take the path on the right beginning at a kissing gate, where a footpath signpost points the way across the fields. After following a hedge on the right in the next field the path veers slightly left (northwest) heading for the canal's Roundthorn Bridge.

Go across the bridge and take the grass track ahead past a farmhouse and through an avenue of birches. Leave this for a wide grass track on the left. On this stretch you'll soon see the vast heathland of **Whixall Moss** on the right.

Turn left at a junction of tracks and return to the canal towpath. Turn right along this before crossing the steel-constructed Roving Bridge by the junction with

Map continues on page 133

the Prees Branch of the **Llangollen (Ellesmere) Canal**. Follow the branch's towpath to Allman's Bridge, which takes the route across the canal and behind a pretty red-bricked cottage. Leave its drive to take a field path

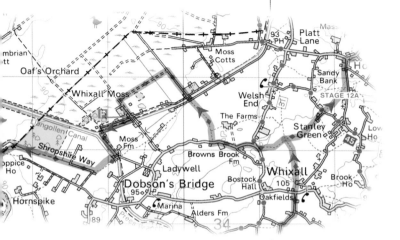

running alongside a dyke on the left. Angle right to Moss Lane Farm and go between the house and a barn before following the farm track ahead (not the one on the left) towards the woods of Bettisfield Moss.

Where the farm track turns left, go straight ahead on a grass track that enters the woods. As it reaches a clearing the Way veers left then, beyond a kissing gate, turns right. Through the trees you should see the red-brick-built Bettisfield Windmill. The track passes some houses before coming to a junction, where you should turn left, then immediately left again, before turning right along a country lane. After 180 metres turn right on a waymarked path angling across fields to the Cornhill Bridge over the Llangollen Canal. The route will now follow the towpath past the villages of **Bettisfield** and then **Hampton Bank** (campsite) and under the B5063 road. ▶

The B-road will also take you to accommodation at nearby Welshampton.

131

*The Llangollen Canal towpath as it passes Blake Mere*

The towpath continues to the first of the big 'meres', **Cole Mere**, and here you leave the canal for a while to cross bridge number 54 before turning right and following the path closer to the shoreline of the mere. The path comes out beyond Limekiln Cottage and turns right to rejoin the canal towpath, which it follows past **Blake Mere**.

Leave the canal on the approach to the tunnel under the A-roads and climb to the A495. Turn left, then right along the footpath of A528, passing **The Mere**.

Go across a pedestrian crossing opposite the Boathouse Café, through a kissing gate opposite, continue half-right on a path climbing the bailey of the old Ellesmere Castle. The path rounds the motte, which now houses a bowling green. Go down some steps, to the left before descending to a narrow lane. Turn right along the lane, passing Love Lane before taking the next left fork, St John's Hill, which descends to High Street in **Ellesmere**. ◄

Note the Georgian houses and the fine old shopfronts of independent traders.

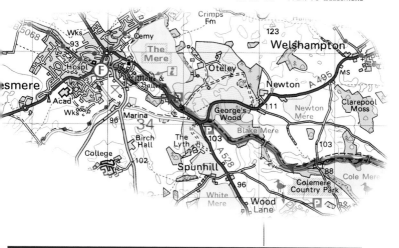

## ELLESMERE

The old Saxon town lies next to an expansive lake, the Mere, one of nine in the area. Like the mosses of the region, the meres were formed in the last Ice Age, when blocks of ice from retreating glaciers formed deep kettle holes in the glacial moraine, thus trapping the water.

It is thought that Norman baron, Roger de Montgomerie, built the motte and bailey castle in the late 11th century and the Knights of St John had St Mary's Church built in 1225. In 1177 Henry II granted the castle and the region to Dafydd ab Owain Gwynedd, ruler of the Welsh kingdom of Gwynedd, who had married his sister, Emme of Anjou. For many years Ellesmere was ruled by the Welsh under Llewelyn the Great, Llewelyn ap Grufydd and Dafydd ap Grufydd. But in 1282 royal troops from Chester took it back for England. The castle is thought to have fallen into disrepair in the 14th century.

The canals and the railway came to Ellesmere following the Industrial Revolution but the railway, which joined the network at Whitchurch and Oswestry, was closed in 1962. Today, the town is an attractive tourist centre with visitors coming to see the meres, mosses and the canal. The Mere is important for migrating birds including smew, teal, goldeneye, pochard and goosander – there's a heronry on an island too.

# STAGE 12A

*Welsh End Corner to Whitchurch (Grindley Brook)*

| | |
|---|---|
| **Start** | Welsh End Corner (SJ 513 352) |
| **Finish** | Grindley Brook Locks |
| **Distance** | 9¾ miles (15.8km); 14½ miles (23.4km) from Wem |
| **Ascent** | 80m; 120m from Wem |
| **Descent** | 95m; 115m from Wem |
| **Time** | 4–5hr; 7hr from Wem |
| **Terrain** | Field paths, country lanes and town streets, canal towpath |
| **Map** | OS Explorer 241, 257 |
| **Supplies** | Wem, Prees Heath, Dodington, Whitchurch |

Highlights of the Whitchurch leg are Prees Heath Common, an old aerodrome returned to heathland, and Brown Moss, a beautiful area of small lanes, woodland and heath. Paths lead to Whitchurch, an historic town offering the traveller refreshment before continuing the short trip to Grindley Locks on the Llangollen Canal. On the way it follows the green corridor that is the Whitchurch Waterways Country Park.

From **Welsh End Corner** junction go over the little footbridge over the dyke and turn right alongside the hedge. Over the next stile head northeast across the fields with the distant brick-built Mill House directly ahead. The path passes to the left of a pond then left of the house before following its drive to a country lane. Go through the gate opposite and continue northeast across a large field, aiming slightly left of the barn of Higher House Farm. Go over a stile in a tall hedge and cut across the corner of the next field before passing well to the left of Higher House Farm and out to the lane. Turn left along the lane, then right at the T-junction (signed to Tilstock and Whitchurch) to pass through the pleasant village of **Hollinwood**, which has a picnic table on its green.

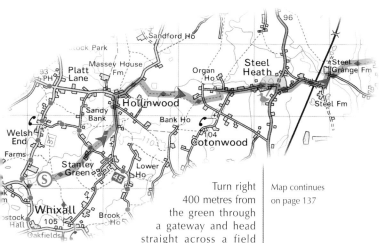

Map continues on page 137

Turn right 400 metres from the green through a gateway and head straight across a field (probably laid with crops). Keep to the right of three large trees in the middle of the field. The route is joined by a tall hedge on the right and bears round to the left to a gated footbridge. Across this, walk alongside a hedge on the left passing Hayes Farm to reach another lane.

Turn right for a few paces then left over a stile to cross a field. The far stile is partially hidden in a hedge, but it lies about 50 metres left of the clearly visible farm gate. Over the stile, maintain direction but, if the field is heavily cropped and with no path cut through the crops, you can follow the left field-edge. A large sycamore tree marks the position of the stile out to the lane on the left. Turn right along the unsurfaced lane then keep left at its junction with a lane that takes the route past the woods of **Steel Heath**.

Turn right at the road junction to follow the B5476 to its first junction. Turn left along the lane, keeping right at the next junction. The winding lane passes over the railway. Just beyond **Steel Grange Farm** leave it and go through a gate on the left. The path angles northeast across the field to the hedge coming in from the right,

135

close to the far corner. Here, go over a gated footbridge and follow the field-edge on the left and to the north of Oak Farm to the busy A49 road.

The route crosses the A49 (take care) and a Shropshire Way sign and two waymarking posts direct you through trees opposite to the main path heading north across **Prees Heath Common**.

> **Prees Heath Common** has been restored from agricultural land and is now a SSSI. It was also used as an airfield in both world wars – the control tower still stands. The sandy sub-soil has been brought to the surface and the heathland, and grassland was re-established by seeding. The silver-studded blue butterfly can be seen on the heather in the second half of June and most of July. The females lay their eggs on ants' nests. The ants guard the egg and the caterpillars for they love the honey-like dew secreted by them.

*On Prees Heath*

The path along the heath passes to the right of some warehouses and to the left of the old aircraft control tower (which has many information boards) before rejoining the road just short of a roundabout. Once again cross the road with care. Turn right along a back road passing several truck-stop cafés, which are also popular with motorcyclists. At the end of this road and in front of the Raven Hotel, a Shropshire Way sign directs you across a dual-carriageway and across the northern part of the heath. Follow the Way on the edge of a crop field at first, then ENE across it in the latter stages to reach a country lane with a triangular grass island. Take the lane ahead to Brown Moss, signed unsuitable for HGVs, then turn left to the entrance of the nature reserve.

Map continues on page 138

**Brown Moss**, formerly a peat bog, is a mixture of marshes, pools, heathland and woodland with a wide variety of flora and fauna. The extremely rare Floating Water Plantain grows in the wetlands and shallow water. There are great crested newts here, too, and you may well see woodpeckers and colourful jays. The moss has been designated as a Local Nature Reserve, SSSI, Special Area of Conservation and Ramsar site.

Take the left-hand waymarked footpath to round the south side of the largest and most southerly lake before following a left fork path which curves right past a smaller lake. On nearing some cottages turn right at a Shropshire Way signpost, then, in a grassy area with a view

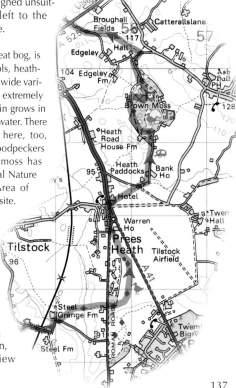

*The main lake at Brown Moss Nature Reserve*

back to the main lake, turn left to follow the path out to a country lane.

Turn left along the lane, before following a right fork signed 'Whitchurch and Ash Magna'. At the first corner take the bridleway path through the gate (not the footpath to the right of it) and follow the hedge. The impressive Edgeley Hall looks down on you from a hill to the left. After the second field turn right along

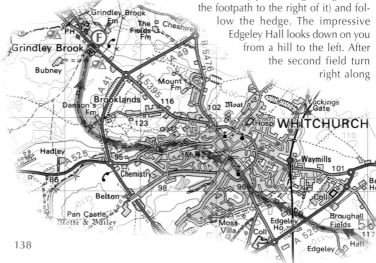

the country lane which comes to the A525 next to a massive warehouse complex. Cross the road with care and continue along the lane ahead, which passes beneath the railway and some sports fields before coming to the Prees Road. Turn right, then take the left fork to pass through Dodington, an historic suburb of **Whitchurch** with some fine half-timbered houses. ▸

Head up Mill Street, which is signed 'A525 Wrexham'. Turn right by the Brookes Court flats before following a walled passageway. After passing a mill that has been converted into a Thai restaurant, follow a tarred path through parkland. Take the right fork path passing

On reaching the pedestrian zone, a right turn will take you to Whitchurch town centre. If you are going to Grindley Brook afterwards you will need to return to this point.

## WHITCHURCH

Founded by the Romans as Mediolanum, 'the place in the mid plain', in AD52, Whitchurch was built on Watling Street between their forts at Chester and Wroxeter. Roman and earlier Iron Age artefacts have been found in the nearby mosses and can be seen at the Whitchurch Heritage Centre.

The Normans built a motte and bailey castle here, also St Alkmund's Church, which was built with a white stone that gave rise to the town's subsequent name, Whitchurch. A second medieval church was built on the same ground but the central tower collapsed in 1711. The majestic red sandstone church that stands today replaced it in 1712.

The town was granted a market charter in the 14th century. Seventeenth-century clockmakers, JB Joyce & Co, gained Whitchurch a reputation for building tower clocks, which can still be seen all around the world. They even helped with the construction of the 'Big Ben' clock in the Palace of Westminster.

The Old Eagles, which dates back to the 14th century, is the oldest building in the town and has a cruck timber-framed construction. Much of this old medieval town house's construction has been obscured by Victorian alterations. Many of the town's fine timber-framed buildings were refaced with the 'more fashionable' brick but newer Georgian buildings have made up for this.

Famous residents of Whitchurch include Sir John Talbot, the first Earl of Shrewsbury and 'the scourge of France', who fought in the hundred years war; 16th-century chancellor Sir Thomas Egerton; and composer Edward German.

through the children's playground out onto a car park. At the far end of the car park cross the road near the mini-roundabout and follow the tarred path off Waterside Close opposite. The stony path, signed 'canal and country park', descends into a ribbon of greenery between houses, many recently built. After crossing a road by one of these estates the stony path continues to reach another, Greenfield Rise after climbing some steps. The route turns left along the road for a short way before turning right again along a waymarked path. Ignoring turnings, follow the path marked 'canal' under a concrete bridge, then a brick one, known as the Chemical Bridge. The canal proper begins now. Follow the towpath to its junction with the Llangollen Canal, where there's a lift bridge.

Go over the lift bridge and turn right along the towpath to reach **Grindley Brook**. The path ends by the seven-tier Grindley Brook Locks and the Lockside Café.

*Grindley Brook Locks*

You can, if you wish, continue on the Sandstone Trail from here. However, if you intend to complete the northern round of the Shropshire Way the Llangollen Canal towpath will take you back to join the route to Ellesmere at Roundthorn Bridge, Whixall Moss (SJ 501 357), a distance of 6 miles (9.7km). Alternatively, you can retrace your steps to Welsh End Corner.

**Reverse direction: Whitchurch to Welsh End Corner**

▶ From the Lockside Café at **Grindley Brook** follow the towpath to the junction with the Llangollen Canal. Here go over the lift bridge and follow the canal to its terminus at the brick-built Chemical Bridge. Beyond the bridge a surfaced path signed 'town' continues beneath a concrete bridge before coming to another road, Greenfield Rise. Turn left along it, cross the bridge over Staggs Brook, then fork right down some steps before following another surfaced path heading east through a grassy valley between houses on the outskirts of **Whitchurch**.

If making Whitchurch the starting point before doing the main circular, ignore the first section from Grindley Brook to Whitchurch.

After crossing the road by a relatively new housing estate (2018) the path continues through the valley to emerge at Waterside Close. Turn left along this for a few metres to a mini-roundabout and cross the road before turning left through a car park. Go through the gates into Jubilee Park, where Shropshire Way waymarks point the way along tarred paths through a children's playground and southeast through the gardens, keeping the bandstand well to the left.

At the end of the park continue on a tarred walled passageway which leads to Mill Street by Brookes Court (flats). Turn left to the mini-roundabout and turn right along Watergate, signed 'A49 Shrewsbury'. ▶ You pass through the historic suburb of Dodington.

If you're stopping in Whitchurch, the town centre is straight on from the mini-roundabout along the pedestrianised street.

Beyond the grand, red-bricked Dodington Lodge the road comes to a mini-roundabout, where the Way turns right, then almost immediately forks left on Edgeley Road, passing sports fields and under a railway bridge. The road ends and becomes a path leading to the busy A525 by a huge factory complex. Cross the road with care and go straight ahead on a country lane. After nearly 400 metres go through a bridleway gate next to a farm gate and follow the hedge-line on the left across a field. Where the hedge veers left head very slightly right and go through the next bridleway gate. By now the impressive **Edgeley Hall** looks down from the hillside on the right. In the next field, again follow the hedge-line on the left to a country lane, where you turn right before turning left at the next junction. This leads to **Brown Moss Nature Reserve**.

Ignore the first minor lane to the right but leave the lane at the next one (SJ 561 398). After a few paces leave the lane for a path on the left passing to the left of a small lake and leading through woodland and out to a clearing. On reaching a picnic area a Shropshire Way sign highlights the path on the right, which leads back into woodland. Turn left on a path that heads south along the edge of the reserve and passes another small lake. Take a left fork, cross a footbridge and pass by the southern shores of the main lake. At the eastern end of the lake take a right fork to reach a lane. Turn right along this past **Bank House** to a T-junction.

Cross the road to a waymarked path straight ahead. This heads southwest along a strip of rough heath on the edge of arable fields to reach the dual-carriageway at **Prees Heath**, close to a large roundabout. Cross with extreme care to the Raven Hotel then turn left on a minor road passing the lorry park and several transport cafés. There's a convenience store in the garage complex here if you need to stock up. The road comes out to the A49 south of the roundabout. Beyond the last building cross the road onto the path across Prees Heath Common (see Prees Heath Common above).

The path gently curves right (south) and keeps to the left of industrial units. ◀ Watch out for the orange Shropshire Way waymarker which points right, back through scrub woodland to the A49. Again, cross this with care and continue along the field-edge path opposite. Go over a gated footbridge, which is staggered to the left at the far end of the field, turn left for a few metres then head southwest across the large field, keeping **Steel**

You may wish to detour left to see the old airfield control tower and its information boards.

**Grange Farm** to the right. Go through the gate and turn right along a winding lane. Cross over the railway bridge, take the left fork, then turn right.

Take the first left lane, passing the woods of **Steel Heath** and follow the right fork lane for around 150 metres. Go over a stile into a field. If there are crops in, turn right and follow the field edge, if not angle half-right to the apex of the hedge then walk alongside it to the stile into the next field. Cross the field and head towards the buildings of Hayes Farm to locate a roadside stile.

Turn right for a few paces to cross the stile on the far side of the lane then follow the hedge on the right. Over a gated footbridge at the far end the Way enters a huge field that is often set to crops. Aim for three large trees in the middle of the field before heading northwest, staying equidistant to Holly Farm and the house to the right. The path comes out to a road at SJ 525 365.

Turn left along the road passing through the pretty hamlet of **Hollinwood**. After passing the green, turn left at the junction. After nearly 400 metres leave the lane for a path on the right, which begins through a farm gate and angles half-right across three fields and keeps right of Higher House Farm and its outbuilding. The path cuts across the corner of a fourth field, passing close to a large tree-enshrouded pond, then heads southwest to a lane-side stile by a farm gate.

Continue along the cul-de-sac lane ahead past Mill House where a short stretch of farm track, the right fork, leads into a large field. Maintain the southwesterly direction across this, passing to the left of a large pond. Over the next stile follow the hedge on the left to the junction of routes at **Welsh End Corner**, where you join the main route to Ellesmere (see Stage 12).

# STAGE 13

*Ellesmere to Llanymynech*

| | |
|---|---|
| **Start** | High Street, Ellesmere |
| **Finish** | Llanymynech crossroads |
| **Distance** | 14 miles (22.4km) |
| **Ascent** | 90m |
| **Descent** | 110m |
| **Time** | 6hr |
| **Terrain** | Field paths, canal towpath |
| **Map** | OS Explorer 240 |
| **Supplies** | Ellesmere, Maesbury Marsh (farm shop), Pant |

Stage 13 is about canals, and you'll be walking them for most of the day. But they are interesting canals, winding through pretty countryside, often dominated by the distant Breidden and Llanymynech hills. With no hills to climb you'll be able to march quite quickly, leaving more time to relax in one of the inns or cafés or to visit the fascinating quarries at Llanymynech. If you have binoculars you might enjoy looking for wildlife on the lovingly restored habitats of the Aston Locks Nature Reserve.

From the High Street in **Ellesmere** follow the direction set by the blue tourist sign for Llangollen Canal and Ellesmere Wharf. This takes you for a short way down Scotland Street before turning left down Wharf Road to the wharf, which is a short leg from the main canal. Follow the towpath which swings right along the main Llangollen Canal.

The fine Georgian red-bricked buildings known as **Beech House** and the adjacent wharf on the canal corner were once the headquarters of the Ellesmere Canal Company. It is believed that engineer Thomas Telford stayed here during the construction of the canal.

The canal meanders through pastureland and passes under a road bridge at **Onston**. At the next bridge a Shropshire Way sign points up some steps away from the canal. ▶ A farm track takes the route past the farmhouse and outbuildings, which lie to the left. The path cuts diagonally across crop fields. Go over a footbridge at SJ 373 322, then angle half-left towards some houses. Go along a track between the houses before turning left at a T-junction and follow the lane around to the bridge over the canal at **Lower Frankton**. Here, you're looking down on the junction between the Montgomery and Llangollen canals.

Turn right along the towpath of the Llangollen Canal and go over the road bridge across it to gain access to the Montgomery Canal towpath. Follow this left

An alternative option is to stay with the canal and the two routes will meet at Lower Frankton.

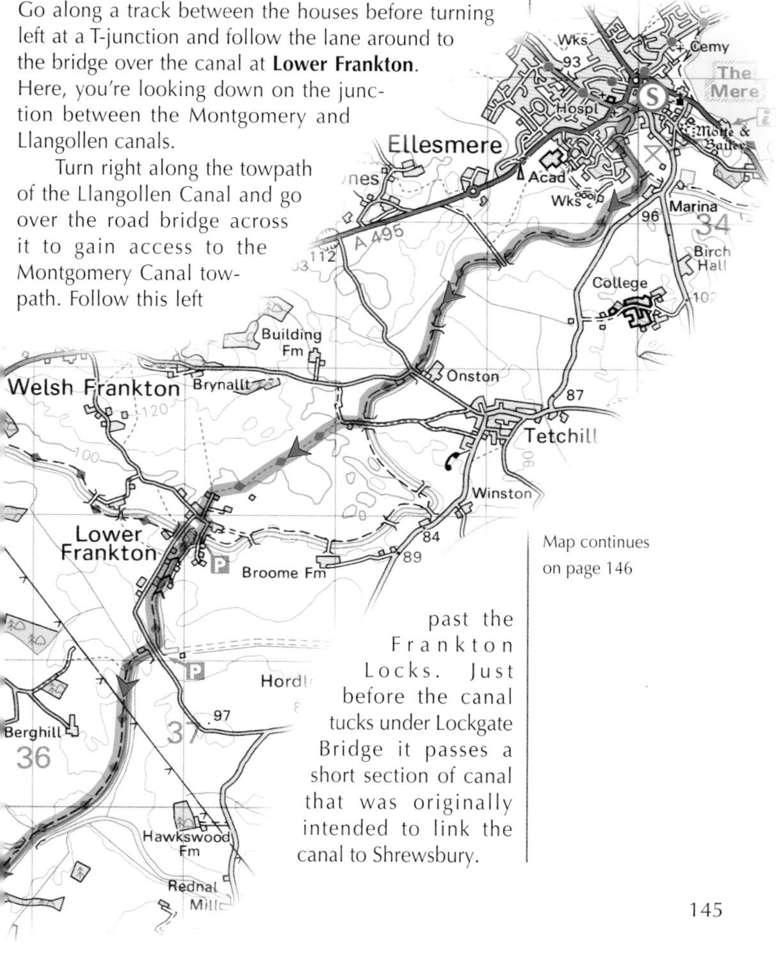

Map continues on page 146

past the Frankton Locks. Just before the canal tucks under Lockgate Bridge it passes a short section of canal that was originally intended to link the canal to Shrewsbury.

145

After a couple of long, straight, tree-lined sections the towpath crosses an old swing bridge over the Rednal Basin before passing beneath the bridge of the Chester to Shrewsbury railway line. Just beyond this it comes to Heath Houses, where the canal bridge should be crossed to access the towpath, which now continues along the other bank. Another long straight ensues and takes the route beneath the two roads at **Queen's Head**, a village that takes its name from the huge pub that towers above the road bridge spanning the canal (refreshment available).

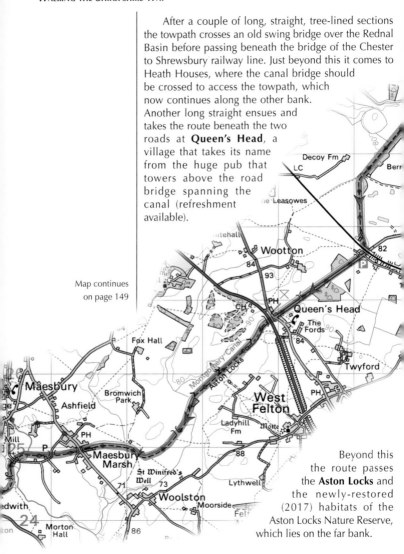

Map continues on page 149

Beyond this the route passes the **Aston Locks** and the newly-restored (2017) habitats of the Aston Locks Nature Reserve, which lies on the far bank.

*Montgomery Canal north of Queen's Head*

The work on **Aston Locks Nature Reserve** is being funded by the Heritage Lottery Fund (HLF) and the European Regional Development Fund (ERDF) and supported by the Montgomery Canal Partnership. Rare aquatic plants, including Floating Water Plantain, have been introduced to the reserve.

After meandering through rolling pastoral countryside, the Way arrives at **Maesbury Marsh**, where there's the Navigation Inn (excellent, if slightly pricey, bar meals). Not far beyond the village the towpath passes the Canal Centre where there's a good café, accommodation, including a campsite, and horse-drawn canal-boat trips.

Beyond the Croft's Mill swing road bridge you'll see a canal arm that used to serve Peate's Mill, then you'll come to the old 'coal' wharf at Gronwen. The canal meanders among pastures beneath the **Redwith Bridge** before coming to Pryce's Bridge (No 84). ▶

In 2018 the canal beyond here was dry although plans are underway to reconstruct the waterway all the way to Newtown in Wales.

## LLANYMYNECH

*Llanymynech on the Welsh border with the plains of the River Vyrnwy and the Breidden Hills on the horizon*

Llanymynech, which in Welsh means blessed place of the monks, lies by the banks of the River Vyrnwy, sheltered in the north by Llanymynech Hill. A huge 57ha fort on the summit of Llanymynech Hill dates back to the Iron Age or possibly late Bronze Age – it is known that the latter tribesmen smelted copper here for their tools and weapons. Later the Romans utilised the mines. A hoard of silver coins and other Roman artefacts were found here. Mining continued in the 12th century for the Bishop of Salisbury, who was trying to raise a ransom to free King Richard the Lionheart.

The Montgomery and adjoining Ellesmere canals reached Llanymynech around 1786 and the transport opportunities they offered became the catalyst in increasing the scale of limestone quarrying and subsequent burning into quicklime. There were two main quarries, the Welsh and the English, each with their own inclines. Lime was transported to wharfs in both Llanymynech and Pant. By the 19th century limestone quarrying became the area's major industry – the huge limestone scars that overlook the town bear testament to this. By 1860 the railways came, leaving the canal and its wharfs to fall into decline. The waterway was breached at this time.

The Hoffman kiln project of 1900, which included more tramways and railway sidings, was the quarry's last major works. The lime-burning kiln, its chimney and two tunnel vaults are remarkably well preserved over 100 years after the closure of the quarries in 1914.

The towpaths are still in good order and lead the Way alongside the vegetation-choked canal channel. The wooded Llynclys Hill ahead and the shapely Breidden Hills across fields to the south become increasingly dominant as the route nears the village of **Pant**, where Cambrian Heritage Railway runs old steam trains to Llynclys.

The canal too has been restored and is water-filled beyond a sluice gate close to the Llanymynech limestone works. Here you can see the old chimney of the lime-burning Hoffman Kiln and the ornate stone-built stable block through the trees. Soon the buildings of Llanymynech come into full view. As you reach the bridge carrying the A483, climb the steps to the road. The crossroads is to the left, as is the Cross Keys Hotel, in the centre of **Llanymynech**.

149

# STAGE 14

*Llanymynech to Nesscliffe*

| | |
|---|---|
| **Start** | Llanymynech crossroads |
| **Finish** | The Old Three Pigeons Inn, Nesscliffe |
| **Distance** | 14¼ miles (23km) |
| **Ascent** | 140m |
| **Descent** | 135m |
| **Time** | 6hr |
| **Terrain** | Field, forest and riverside paths, country lanes |
| **Map** | OS Explorer 240 |
| **Supplies** | Llanymynech, Nesscliffe (filling station/shop) |
| **Notes** | The Nesscliff training area is generally used for dry training (ie no live firing), however, there are biannual exercises held that involve the firing of battle simulation charges. During such exercises access over the public footpaths is controlled. For information, tel 01743 741607. The riverside paths by the Afon Efyrnwy (River Vyrnwy) are prone to flooding during the winter months. |

Llanymynech is the start of the home run to Shrewsbury. For much of the morning the Shropshire Way follows the flood barrier of the River Vyrnwy, which meanders like a snake on the move. Melverley, the first village encountered, is lovely with its black and white half-timbered church and pretty cottages. The fields beyond are set mainly to crop but for most of the time the walking is easy. Nesscliffe Hill is in sight for some time, getting nearer and nearer. And then you're on its summit, looking back on your day's walk, which is laid out beneath your feet like a map.

From the crossroads in the centre of **Llanymynech** take the B4398 signed 'Knockin'. After 1000 metres, opposite the drive of Lower House Farm, turn right through a farm gate and head south across a narrow field. The gap in the tall hedge used by the footpath at the far end of the field is nearer the right edge than is shown on current

(2018) maps. The path now heads south across a large field heading for the River Vyrnwy. ▶

The path traces the river on fields used by equestrians – you'll see the jumps to your left. The path misses out the big loop in the river by Rhandregynwen Farm (opposite bank) and instead cuts a corner following old flood embankments. The path will follow these embankments known locally as the Argae for several miles. The river loops back in but the embankment still guides the route to a footbridge. Go straight on through a gate rather than following the path beyond a stile on the left. The embankment leads across more fields.

Cross the unsurfaced lane south of **Dyfrydd** and continue along the embankment. Over a step-stile the Way crosses a lawned area with the River Morda to the left then comes to two cottages marked Mill House on the OS Explorer 1:25,000 map. Go through a farm gate and along a paved drive to pass between buildings, then turn right over a ladder stile to pass through a rather overgrown ginnel. This leads back to the embankment. Turn left along it. The modest, red-bricked **Pentreheylin Hall** can now be seen on the left. As the embankment meets a road turn left over a stile then right along the road for

In summer some of the stiles can be obscured by hedges and rarely in the early stages do you glimpse the river itself, which hides behind trees and thick vegetation.

*Ancient church at Melverley*

151

a short way before returning to the embankment at the next gate.

The path meanders with the river and approaches **Melverley**, passing between the river and the campsite before entering the churchyard by a pretty black and white half-timbered church. Turn left along a lane to a T-junction by what used to be the Tontine Inn.

Go over a stile in the hedge opposite and head diagonally left (NNE) across a field then across the grassy rake of a dismantled railway. Maintain direction across

the next field
following the hedge on the right
to reach a lane at SJ 335 169. Go over the stile on the opposite side to cross three more fields, still in a NNE direction. Go over a stile in the right-hand corner of the last field before turning right along a lane past the cottages of Ponthen. Turn right at the next junction, then left just before the Royal Hill pub and campsite.

After about 70 metres go over a stile on the right and cross two fields. The second, which has a large pond in it, is overgrown. Over another stile the path maintains its easterly direction across a campsite before crossing a larger field out onto a country lane. The field path across the lane and through a gate is staggered to the right. It angles slightly right across several fields, coming out at a road after passing to the left of the Firs.

Turn left along the lane, following it around the first bend. At the second bend leave the lane for a path following a drive past the corner house and its garages then along a grassy area into fields. The path comes to a disused railway trackbed by the edge of the **Military Training Area**.

The **Nesscliff Training Camp**, built on the site of the Central Ammunition Depot, was opened in 1941 by the War Office. Here ammunition was stored in bunkers. The site covered an extensive area to avoid possible devastation of an accidental explosion or attack by the enemy. The ammunition was stored in bunkers hewn in the rocks. To service the depot the War Office commandeered the ailing Shrewsbury and Montgomery Railway known locally as the Potts Line – you'll walk a short section of it before entering the camp. The depot closed in 1959 but the bunkers are used in exercises. Strangely the modern camp has omitted the 'e' from the name Nesscliffe.

Map continues on page 156

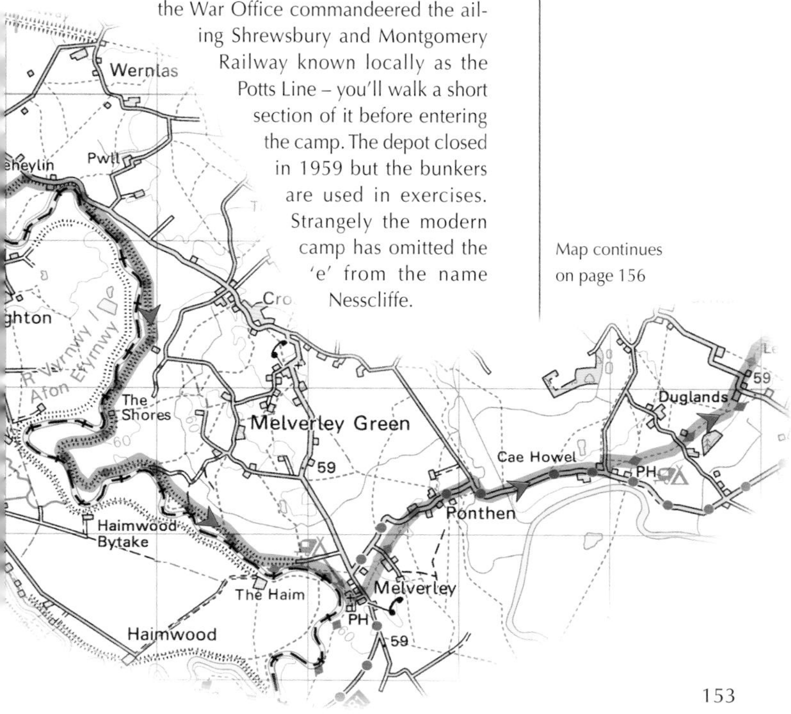

153

Oliver's Point, Nesscliffe Hill

Turn right along the old railway. After 250 metres fork left along a grassy track that curves left through a strip of woodland to a step-stile by a gate. Over this cross a military track and follow the left field-edge ahead to another stile into woodland. At the time of writing this new path was faint in the middle stretches but waymarking is being added by the Shropshire Way Association and the council. The path heads northeast and crosses a plank bridge over a dry ditch at SJ 366 186 and soon becomes ingrained on the ground. It turns left for a few paces then crosses a step-stile before going over an isolated stile (no fence) onto a military track. Turn right, then left after a few paces along another track, which curves left with woods on the left and the brick bunkers of the training ground on the right.

The track soon passes to the right of the huge expanse of the main training area, then draws alongside a wood on the right. Go through the metal farm-type gate on the right and take the right one of two narrow paths through the trees. The path draws close to an old wire fence on the right as it heads NNE near the woodland edge. A short grassy track on the right takes the route out of the woods onto a grassy strip, from where you'll see the gate through some trees at the northern edge of the training area. Beyond the gate, follow a pleasant green lane to the road at **Kinton**.

Turn left along the road past Kinton House and follow it around to the right. Go straight ahead at the next junction and follow the winding lane over the bridge spanning the A5 dual-carriageway to a T-junction. The signed path is staggered to the right across the road and follows a hedge before maintaining direction across open crop fields. Having entered the third field (SJ 378 207) turn right, now with a hedge on the right, go over a stile and continue across more crop fields with the conifer-clad Hopton Hill directly ahead and that of Nesscliffe slightly to the right. The path comes out to a lane beneath Hopton Hill. Turn right here, ignoring side roads and follow the lane south past the houses of **Hopton**.

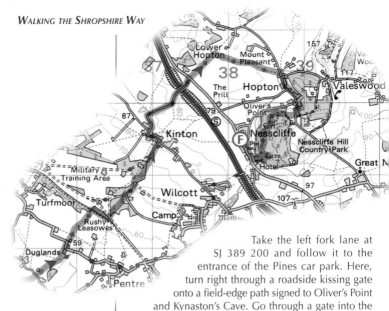

Take the left fork lane at SJ 389 200 and follow it to the entrance of the Pines car park. Here, turn right through a roadside kissing gate onto a field-edge path signed to Oliver's Point and Kynaston's Cave. Go through a gate into the woods of **Nesscliffe Hill Country Park**.

Turn right on a bridleway path signed Oliver's Point. At the next junction fork left, climbing into an open area and through the ramparts of an old Iron Age fort to the Oliver's Point summit viewpoint, where you look westwards through the pines and across the plains of the Severn to the distinctive peaks of the Breidden Hills.

The path then curves round left, through the ramparts of the old fort to reach a picnic area. Follow the path signed to Kynaston's Cave. This traces the western rim of the hill before passing above some fencing at the top of a sandstone quarry and descending steeply in steps by more fencing. The path comes down to the base of the sandstone cliffs then turns right to **Kynaston's Cave**.

Beyond the cave the path descends left to a lower bridleway, where you should turn left, then right to the woodland edge. Ignore the bridleway gate on the left and go over the stile to the right of it on a path tracing the woodland edge. Descend steps to a drive leading past an

## NESSCLIFFE HILL

Kynaston's Cave, Nesscliffe

The wooded sandstone escarpment of Nesscliffe Hill is topped by the remains of an Iron Age fort whose earthwork ramparts are visible from the summit viewpoint. At one time it would have resounded to the sound of quarrying for this superb red sandstone, which helped to build many of the region's castles, churches and public buildings. Today it's a place of leisure and discovery. The Shropshire Way explores the impressive cliffs formed by the quarrying. Carved steps lead upwards to a two-chambered cave halfway up the cliffs. This was home for many years to a notorious highwayman, Sir Humphrey Kynaston.

Kynaston was a fast-living gentleman who had inherited Myddle Castle from his father, the High Sheriff of Shropshire. He was convicted of murder in 1491 but was later pardoned. Debt forced him to abandon the castle and he set up home in the cave with his horse, Beelzebub. Here, he lived a Robin Hood type life, robbing from the rich and giving to the poor. The hill was a known meeting place for highway robbers and travellers were extremely reluctant to come this way. Some say Kynaston became ill and died in the cave in 1534; others say, after a pardon in 1516, he ended his days in comfort, somewhere in Welshpool. The cave was subsequently inhabited until the 18th century. These days the cave is a protected home for Pipistrelle, Daubenton's and Natterer's bats.

old sandstone building that was once a school (note the clock on its roof). Across a tarred yard the route comes to the main road in **Nesscliffe**. Turn right to reach the Old Three Pigeons Inn.

# STAGE 15

*Nesscliffe to Shrewsbury*

| | |
|---|---|
| **Start** | The Old Three Pigeons Inn, Nesscliffe |
| **Finish** | Kingsland Bridge, Shrewsbury |
| **Distance** | 12 miles (19.4km) |
| **Ascent** | 165m |
| **Descent** | 200m |
| **Time** | 5–6hr |
| **Terrain** | Field and riverside paths, country lanes |
| **Map** | OS Explorer 240, 241 |
| **Supplies** | Nesscliffe (filling station/shop), Shrewsbury |

The last day and again it's a leisurely one, across fields, by riverbanks and finally back through historic Shrewsbury. By now, if you didn't know before, you may be recognising individual cereal crops and the difference between wheat and maize. You'll find that the Shrawardine Castle on the map isn't Shrawardine Castle and that Shrawardine is a delectable Severnside chocolate box village. From Shelton onwards, the Severn will be your guide as it loops around Shrewsbury to journey's end by Kingsland Bridge.

*A cottage at Shrawardine*

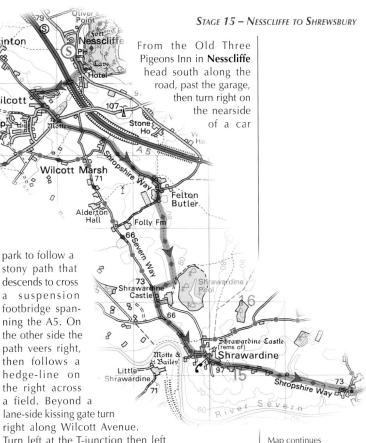

From the Old Three Pigeons Inn in **Nesscliffe** head south along the road, past the garage, then turn right on the nearside of a car park to follow a stony path that descends to cross a suspension footbridge spanning the A5. On the other side the path veers right, then follows a hedge-line on the right across a field. Beyond a lane-side kissing gate turn right along Wilcott Avenue. Turn left at the T-junction then left again at another. At a crossroads go straight ahead on the lane signed to Felton Butler and Shrawardine. Follow this for just over a mile to the hamlet of **Felton Butler**.

Where the lane turns sharp left leave it to go through the smaller of two iron gates ahead. The larger one on the left has a security keypad. Follow the unsurfaced vehicle track to the left of the buildings. It turns right at a pond, then left again. Take the right fork track next to head south across fields that may well be sown with

Map continues on page 160

159

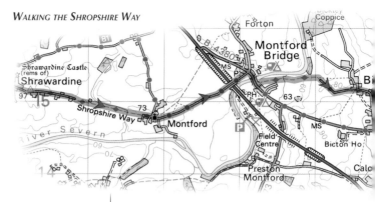

Although the farmhouse you passed earlier called itself Shrawardine Castle, the remains of the real castle lie in a field to the east of the village. There's also a motte and bailey at Little Shrawardine.

crops. The easiest way to find the partially concealed stile in the hedge at the far end is to follow the hedge on the left all the way around the field. Once over the stile follow the left edge of the next two fields. On the approach to Shrawardine Castle Farm you come to a stile where the paths are signed to the right. The way is actually over the stile then right to follow the hedge-side to a lane. Turn left here and follow it to the lovely village of **Shrawardine**, where the lane turns left to pass a charming half-timbered thatched house, the old courthouse and St Mary's Church. ◄

Turn right on the lane beyond the church, then left by Shrawardine Farm along a narrow lane that degenerates into a stony lane. This leads to the village of **Montford**. Turn left by the church then right along a lane for nearly a mile before crossing a bridge over the A5 and into the village of **Montford Bridge**. Turn right at the junction here to cross the River Severn.

On reaching the Wingfield Arms turn left on a short stony track by the side of Farringford House, then, through a gate, head east across a field behind the houses of the Crescent. Go over a footbridge and continue east. The path comes to a junction. The Shropshire Way angles right on an enclosed track that can be very muddy in the middle stages. If you are doing this outside the summer months, it might be better to take the field path ahead instead. Turn right along the lane if you used the field

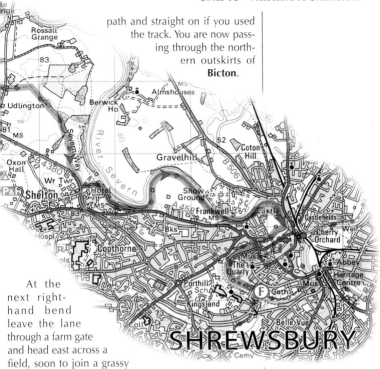

path and straight on if you used the track. You are now passing through the northern outskirts of **Bicton**.

At the next right-hand bend leave the lane through a farm gate and head east across a field, soon to join a grassy track that takes the route past Grove Farm, whose drive leads to a lane by Rossall Lodge (bungalow). Go through a small gate to the right of the white-washed bungalow's drive then up a tightly enclosed ginnel. Continue through a gate and alongside the field edge to the next gate. After veering slightly left to an enclosure with a pond in it, head ESE to the apex of the far field boundary. Slightly to the right go through two adjacent gates, ignoring a stile on the left just beyond. The route now follows the line of the hedge. Join the track coming in from the left for a short distance, then leave it where it turns sharp right. Trace the western edge of Spring Coppice on a field path, then go through the gate straight

*The River Severn near Shelton*

ahead to pass between two woods and join an enclosed track leading out to the B4380 road on the outskirts of **Shelton**. Turn left long the road.

After 100 metres turn left along a woodland track running behind houses and eventually parallel with the **River Severn**. The path briefly joins a road behind a housing estate then turns left again on a path which soon descends steps down to the river. Follow the delightful riverside path round a loop, continue across Doctor's Field Countryside Site.

The path passes beneath the Mount, Charles Darwin's childhood home, then climbs some steps to a road-end. Turn left here to continue along a narrow path above the river then turn left down more steps to return to the riverbank. Follow the riverside path ignoring a path going half-right to a gate in a hedge. ◄

The path on the right traces an old canal built to help boats avoid the shallows of the river ahead.

Pass a footbridge spanning the river and continue on the same side of the river under the Welsh Bridge and up Water Lane. Turn left and at the Porthill footbridge continue along the footpath without crossing the bridge. This will take you past Shrewsbury School and the boathouses. A set of steps will take you up to the south end of Kingsland Bridge in the centre of **Shrewsbury**.

# STRETTON SKYLINE WALK

| | |
|---|---|
| **Start/finish** | The Batch NT car park All Stretton (SO 456 955) |
| **Distance** | 19½ miles (31.4km) |
| **Ascent** | 1320m |
| **Time** | 10–12hr |
| **Terrain** | Steep hill paths, grass and heather ridges and country lanes |
| **Map** | OS Explorer 217 |
| **Refreshment** | Two pubs at Little Stretton |

This 20-miler takes in the peaks that the Shropshire Way dropped but no Shropshire walking book should be without. These are the near-perfect ridges where you can stride out and appreciate what Shropshire has to offer. Caer Caradoc has fine dolerite crags and a huge fairly well-preserved Iron Age fort on top, while the Long Mynd is rent with wonderful coombes, or batches as the locals know them. And they're supplemented by the ridges of Ragleth, Hope Bowdler and the Lawley. If 20 miles is too much Church Stretton lies in the middle, so you can break the walk into two days.

From the car park follow the lane westwards through the Batch in **All Stretton**, crossing the footbridge next to the ford. The lane soon becomes a stony track, delving into the beautiful, steep-sided valley. Beyond a cottage

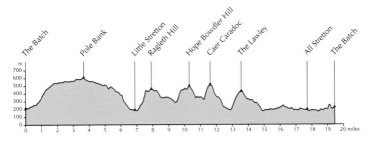

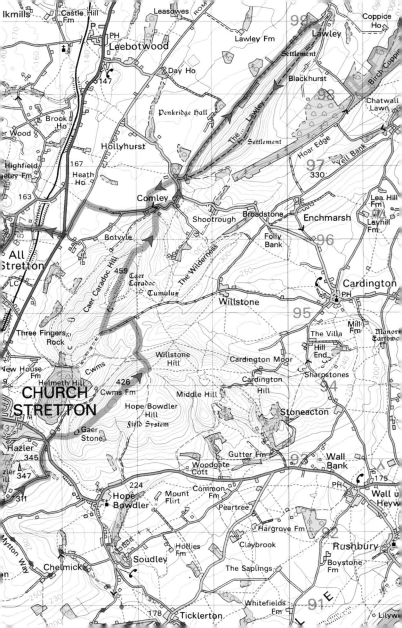

known as **The Batch** the tracks divide. Take the right fork, which goes over a small footbridge over a streamlet and heads north.

Follow the grassy valley track, ignoring the upper right fork beyond a gate. The lower track soon veers left in front of the modern timber house, Robin's Lye. At a 4-way intersection of paths, go straight ahead on the most prominent path that soon bends right into Jonathan's Hollow. The rock and gorse-scattered, steep-sided valley snakes through towards the ridge.

Stay with the valley path ignoring paths to both left and right. The path passes to the left of the most northerly visible earthwork section of Cross Dyke, a Bronze Age border. Beyond this the valley becomes shallow and the path joins a wider track with the fields of High Park not far to the right. Take the less prominent right fork track at SO 439 967, where the track gets closest to the fields. This veers away from the field-edge and, after 800 metres, draws close to a tarred road at Dunkley Nap. Just before meeting the road the track joins a stony ridge track, the ancient Portway, and follows it south-westwards across the heather.

Stay with the ridge track as it heads southwest across the broad, heather-clad ridge. You'll pass a modern shooting box, which has been constructed on top of a Bronze Age tumulus. Just beyond that the track crosses another high lane straddling the ridge. The summit, known as **Pole Bank**, lies about a mile beyond this.

> On **Pole Bank** there's a trig point and a view indicator. On a clear day you can see across the hills of Mid Wales to Snowdonia but nearer at hand are the serrated crags of the Stiperstones and the steep-sided Corndon Hill, which lies just over the Welsh border.

The wide track continues through the heather to reach another lane, which should now be followed south past the tree-surrounded shack marked on the map as **Pole Cottage**. Take the faint grassy path opposite, which soon becomes more prominent. This leads to a

*Pole Bank, the
Long Mynd*

well-defined track heading southeast and staying on the north side of **Round Hill**. Take the left fork track, which gives views into Ashes Hollow before descending to the old earthwork border dyke on Barrister's Plain. From here you get a good view down stony Barrister's Batch and across Callow Hollow to the steep-sided Minton Hill, whose grassy folds are sparsely scattered with small, wind-warped trees. The track follows the rim of Barrister's Batch and onto a saddle between the hills of Grindle and Callow before angling down the beautiful, more verdant Small Batch. ▶

You can see down Small Batch to the rooftops of Little Stretton and across to the next objective, Ragleth Hill.

The track fords the stream as it approaches Small Batch Farm and its campsite. Follow the lane beyond, then take the first left. This comes out at the Ragleth Arms in **Little Stretton**, where you should turn right, passing the black and white half-timbered church. On reaching the Green Dragon pub turn left along Crown Lane, which leads to the busy A49. Turn right here, following the near-side pavement.

After 130 metres turn left along a lane before taking the first left fork past a chalet. Where the track ends follow a path through a grassy hollow and between two woods. It gradually bends left to climb the really steep grassy slopes to the pole on the south summit of **Ragleth Hill**.

A good ridge path heads northeast over the true summit to the northern end, where you get good views of Church Stretton and Caer Caradoc. Ignore a left fork path but turn sharp right with **Ragleth Wood** below you and to the left. Over a couple of stiles, the path comes to a stony farm track, which leads to a high lane. Turn left and follow the lane beneath the slopes of **Hazler Hill** to reach the B4371 Church Stretton to Much Wenlock road.

Cross the road, then go up the drive ahead towards Gaerstones Farm, but turn right before the farmhouse on an extremely steep path with a hedge on the right and a

*The Gaer Stone*

great crag on the horizon. Go over a stile at the top of the field and continue up to the ridge just to the right of that crag, the **Gaer Stone**. Turn left along the rising ridge, past the crag. ▶

After striding out over two cairned summits you come to a cross-fence with a stile in it. Don't go over but descend left here to a grassy saddle and an intersection of paths by a gate (SO 480 945).

Go through the gate and follow the grass bridleway path skirting the right shoulder of a small grassy hill, which partially obscures Caer Caradoc. The path follows the line of the OS Explorer's black dashes rather than the green ones. It joins a stony track, the Cwms Road, where you should turn left. After 400 metres leave the track and turn right, through a kissing gate just beyond a farm gate. This leads onto a path climbing steadily through grass and bracken towards Caer Caradoc's summit. The path soon comes across the impressive dark volcanic rocks overlooking the east side of the hill and the earthworks of the Iron Age fort's outer ramparts. Continue the climb by the ramparts then fork left to the summit of **Caer Caradoc**.

Views are now superb with Caer Caradoc soaring above the Cwms valley and the Long Mynd peeping out from behind the wooded Helmeth Hill and Caer Caradoc's southern slopes.

## CAER CARADOC

Caer Caradoc sits alongside the Church Stretton Fault, part of a great rift that stretched from Cheshire to southwest Wales, the dividing line between two tectonic plates. The one in the west sank beneath the one in the east forcing it upwards and forming sedimentary deposits that built up to form what we now know as the Long Mynd. The heat that ensued brought about the volcanic action that formed the crags of Caer Caradoc and surrounding hills east of the fault.

The summit is also crowned by a large Iron Age Fort with multiple ramparts overlooking precipitous slopes. The fort was named after Caradoc (or Caractacus in Roman), a British chieftain who, along with his armies of Ordovician and Silurian soldiers, resisted the Romans under the rule of Claudius for over a decade. Legend has it that Caradoc fought his final battle on this mountain, one in which he was defeated by the Roman general, Ostorius Scapula. He is said to have fled to a cave on the western slopes below the summit.

*Walking on the fort walls on Caer Caradoc*

Descend the northern slopes. On the approach to the saddle beneath Little Caradoc the path draws alongside a fence on the right. Over a stile in the cross-fence take the path slanting up Little Caradoc. Descend northwards to a fence along the edge of the access land then go left to meet a track that has skirted the west side of the hill. Go through a gate on the right by an information board and follow a track out to a country lane. Turn right on the winding lane through **Comley**.

Go straight ahead at a road junction, then right along the drive to Comley Farm, following it right then left. The route is now going to take the low track along the western side of **The Lawley**, saving the delectable ridge route for later. You'll see the half-timbered **Penkridge Hall** on the left before passing Well House and its stables.

Watch out for a narrow shortcut path at SO 503 989, raking up slopes to the right and alongside woodland – the path marked is with black dashes on the OS Explorer maps. The path meets the one to the **Lawley ridge** just above a roadside car park. Turn sharp right and follow this onto open hillside.

The undulating grassy path passes through bracken that cloaks the steep hillsides. The summit is capped by a pole with a bird and a compass point indicator on top. Follow the descending ridge south-westwards before arcing right near the end to go through a gate close to a farm outbuilding. Beyond this you meet the outward route and follow it along the farm track and out past Comley Farm to the road.

Go up the steps on the opposite side of the road and follow the clear, waymarked field path back to the lane at the foot of Little Caradoc. Turn right along the lane before turning right again along a farm track. Where the track ends, maintain direction across the left edge of another field to reach a narrow country lane. Turn left along this to reach the busy A49. The lane wanted next is staggered slightly left along the road and leads to the B-road just north of All Stretton. Turn left here and follow the road for 340 metres before turning right on a signed bridleway track. You should soon abandon this for a footpath on the left which goes behind cottages and St Michael's and All Angel's Church before coming out along a stony track close to its junction with a lane. Turn left along the lane then right at a T-junction. At the first corner, take a signed footpath on the right. This soon climbs through woodland before turning left and descending back into the Batch. Turn right on reaching the lane and follow it back to the car park.

On the Lawley

# APPENDIX A

*Facilities table*

| Stage | Place | Stage distance | Cumulative distance | Facilities |
|-------|-------|----------------|---------------------|------------|
| 1 | Shrewsbury | | 0 | Numerous hotels, B&Bs, shops |
| 1 | Bayston Hill (A5/A49 services) | 2¼ miles (3.4km) | 2¼ miles (3.4km) | Travelodge, shops, cafés, accessed by paths opposite Pulley Hall (not shown on map) |
| 1 | Bayston Hill | ½ mile (0.9km) | 2¾ miles (4.3km) | Shops, pubs |
| 1 | Wilderley | 5½ miles (8.8km) | 8¼ miles (13.1km) | B&B |
| 1, 2 | Bridges | 6½ miles (10.7km) | 14¾ miles (23.8km) | Youth hostel, inn |
| 2, 3 | Bishop's Castle | 11½ miles (18.5km) | 26¼ miles (42.3km) | Hotels, B&B, camping, shops, cafés |
| 3, 4 | Clun | 10¾ miles (17.4km) | 37 miles (59.7km) | Hotels, youth hostel, cafés, shops |
| 4 | Hopesay | 8 miles (12.9km) | 45 miles (72.6km) | Café |
| 4 | *Aston-on-Clun off route from Hopesay* | *1½ miles (2.4km)* | *46½ miles (75km)* | *Campsite, shop, pub* |
| 4, 5 | Craven Arms | 3¼ miles (5.2km) | 48¼ miles (77.8 km) | Inn (with accommodation), B&B, shops |
| 5 | Bromfield | 8¾ miles (14.2km) | 57 miles (92km) | Hotel/restaurant, shops/café (Ludlow Food Centre) |
| 5, 6 | Ludlow | 1½ miles (2.4km) | 58½ miles (94.4km) | Many hotels, inns, shops, B&Bs |
| 6, 7 | Wheathill | 10¼ miles (15.6km) | 68¾ miles (110km) | Pub (taxi to and from Ludlow or Bridgnorth is best option) |
| 7, 8 | Wilderhope | 11¼ miles (19km) | 80 miles (129km) | Youth hostel |
| 8 | Much Wenlock | 7½ miles (12.1km) | 87½ miles (141.1km) | Hotels, B&Bs, campsites, shops |

| Stage | Place | Stage distance | Cumulative distance | Facilities |
|---|---|---|---|---|
| 8, 9 | Ironbridge | 5 miles (8.1km) | 92½ miles (149.2km) | Hotels, B&Bs, shops, youth hostel (Coalbrookdale) |
| 9 | Little Wenlock | 4½ miles (7.3km) | 97 miles (156.5km) | Hotel |
| 9, 10 | Wellington | 6½ miles (10.4km) | 103½ miles (166.9km) | Hotels, B&Bs, shops |
| 10 | Rodington | 7 miles (11.3km) | 110½ miles (178.2km) | Pub |
| 10, 10A, 11 | Haughmond | 5 miles (8.1km) | 115½ miles (186.3km) | Hotel (Upton Magna), campsites |
| *11* | *Uffington (off route from Haughmond Abbey)* | *1¼ miles (2km)* | *116¾ miles (188.3km)* | *hotel* |
| 11 | Hadnall | 6 miles (9.7km) | 121½ miles (196km) | Shop, pub |
| 11, 12 | Wem | 5¾ miles (9.2km) | 127¼ miles (205.2 km) | Hotel, B&Bs, shops |
| *12* | *Edstaston (off route)* | *0.4 miles (0.7km)* | *131 miles (211.2km)* | *B&B* |
| 12, 13 | Ellesmere | 14½ miles (23.4km) | 141¾ miles (228.6km) | Hotel, B&Bs, shops, cafés |
| 12A | Whitchurch | 14½ miles (23.4km) | 141¾ miles (228.6km) | Hotel, B&B, cafés, shops |
| 13 | Maesbury Marsh | 10¾ miles (17.4km) | 152½ miles (246km) | Pub, campsite, café, |
| 13, 14 | Llanymynech | 3¼ miles (5.2km) | 155¾ miles (251.2km) | Hotel, shops, café |
| 14 | Melverley | 9¼ miles (14.9km) | 165 miles (266.1km) | Campsite, B&B |
| 14, 15 | Nesscliffe | 5 miles (7.9km) | 170 miles (274km) | Pub, apartment |
| 15 | Montford Bridge | 7 miles (11.5km) | 177 miles (285.5km) | Campsite, pub |
| 15 | Shrewsbury | 5 miles (8km) | 182 miles (293.5km) | Numerous hotels, B&Bs, shops |

# APPENDIX B

*Accommodation*

The best website for campsites is
www.ukcampsite.co.uk.

A good all-round comparison site is
www.trivago.co.uk.

The Shropshire Way Association has an
up-to-date accommodation list on their
website: https://shropshireway.org.uk.

Most options listed below are on the
Shropshire Way but some are off route.
These are shown in italics. CL campsites
means certified location and they are
usually exclusive to club members.

## Stage 1 Shrewsbury to Bridges

Just a small selection:

Darwin's Townhouse
37 St Julian's Friars
Shrewsbury
tel 01743 343829
www.darwinstownhouse.com

The Loopy Shrew Hotel
15/17 Bellstone
Shrewsbury
tel 01743 366505
www.loopyshrew.com

The Old Post Office
1 Milk Street
Shrewsbury
tel 01743 236019
www.oldpostofficepub.co.uk

The Lion Hotel
Wyle Cop
Shrewsbury
tel 01743 353107
www.thelionhotelshrewsbury.com

Travelodge
Bayston Hill
tel 08719 846103
www.travelodge.co.uk

Upper Shadymoor Farm (B&B and
glamping)
Nr Wilderley
SJ 454 021
tel 01743 718670
www.shadymoor.co.uk

Brow Farm campsite
Ratlinghope
SO 403 968
tel 01588 650641
www.browfarmcampsite.co.uk

Bridges Long Mynd Youth Hostel
Ratlinghope
SO 395 965
tel 01588 650656
email bridges@yha.org.uk

The Bridges
(formerly the Horseshoes Inn)
tel 01588 650260
http://thebridgespub.co.uk

## Stage 2 Bridges to Bishop's Castle

*Inn on the Green*
*Wentnor*
*(2½ miles off route from Linley)*
*tel 01588 650105*

*The Coach House*
*Norbury*
*SO 364 928*
*(1 mile east of Linley)*
*tel 01588 650846*
*www.coachhousenorbury.com*

Foxholes Castle Bunkhouse and
Campsite
Above Bishop's Castle
SO 324 897
tel 01588 638924
www.foxholes-castle.co.uk

The Castle Hotel
Bishop's Castle
tel 01588 638403
www.thecastlehotelbishopscastle.co.uk

Bank House B&B
4 High Street
Bishop's Castle
tel 01588 630026
www.bishopscastlebedandbreakfast.co.uk

Curly Tail Accommodation
Boar's Head
Church Street
Bishop's Castle
tel 01588 638521
www.boarsheadhotel.co.uk

**Stage 3 Bishop's Castle to Clun**
Middle Woodbatch Farm (B&B and
camping)
SO 298 882
tel 01588 630141
www.middlewoodbatchfarm.co.uk

White Horse Inn
The Square
Clun
tel 01588 418144
www.whi-clun.co.uk

The Sun Inn
High Street
Clun
tel 01588 640559

Clun (The Mill) Youth Hostel
SO 303 812
tel 0345 3719112
email: clunmill@yha.org.uk

**Stage 4 Clun to Craven Arms**
*Wayside Camping*
*Aston-on-Clun*
*SO 399 817*
*(1½ miles south of Hopesay)*
*tel 01588 660218*
www.waysidecamping.co.uk

Stokesay Inn
Craven Arms
tel 01588 672304
www.thestokesayinn.com

**Stage 5 Craven Arms to Ludlow**
*Castle View B&B*
*A49 Stokesay*
*(½ mile south off route near Craven Arms)*
*tel 01588 673712*
www.castleviewstokesay.co.uk

The Clive Arms
Bromfield
tel 01588 856565
www.theclive.co.uk

Ludlow Mascall Centre (hostel)
Lower Galdeford
Ludlow
tel 01584 873882
www.ludlowmascallcentre.co.uk

Whitcliffe Campsite
Ludlow
SO 501 743
tel 01584 872026
www.northfarmludlow.co.uk/
whitcliffe.html

### Stage 6 Ludlow to Wheathill
The Graig
Angel Bank
Clee Hill
tel 01584 890 204
www.thegraigludlow.co.uk

The Timberstone
Cleestanton
tel 01584 823519
www.timberstoneludlow.co.uk

*The Pheasant*
*Neenton*
*(5-mile taxi ride north of route at*
*Wheathill)*
*tel 01746 787955*
www.pheasantatneenton.co.uk

### Stage 7 Wheathill to Wilderhope Manor (Wenlock Edge)
*The Crown Hotel*
*Munslow*
*SO 521 873*
*(3 miles off route)*
*tel 01584 841205*
www.crowncountryinn.co.uk

Sky View Guest House
Wood Farm
Near Longville-in-the Dale
SO 535 949
tel 01694 771427

Wilderhope Manor
Longville-in-the-Dale
Wenlock Edge
SO 544 928
tel 0345 3719149
email: wilderhope@yha.org.uk

### Stage 8 Wilderhope (Wenlock Edge) to Ironbridge
*Mill Farm Holiday Park and B&B*
*Hughley*
*SO 564 979*
*(1 mile off route at Ippikin's Rock,*
*Wenlock Edge)*
*tel 01746 785208*
https://millfarmholidaypark.com

*Easthope Camping and Caravan site*
*(1 mile off route at Easthope Woods,*
*Wenlock Edge)*
*tel 01746 785434*
www.easthopecaravanandcamping.
co.uk

Lower Hill Farm Campsite
Presthope
Wenlock Edge
SO 581 978
tel 01746 785292
www.lowerhillcampsite.co.uk

Stokes Barn Bunkhouse
Much Wenlock
SO 609 999
tel 01952 727491
www.stokesbarn.co.uk

The Sytche Caravan & Camping
Much Wenlock
SJ 619 004
tel 01952 726701
www.sytchecaravanandcamping.co.uk

The Manor House B&B
Sheinton Street
Much Wenlock
tel 01952 728046
www.muchwenlockbandb.co.uk

The Raven Hotel
Much Wenlock
tel 01952 727251
www.ravenhotel.com

The White Hart
Ironbridge
tel 01952 432901
www.whitehartironbridge.com

The Malthouse
Ironbridge
tel 01952 433712
http://themalthouseironbridge.co.uk

Riverside B&B
Ironbridge
tel 01952 433283

The Foundry Master House
Coalbrookdale
tel 01952 433658
www.thefoundrymastershouse.co.uk

*Ironbridge Coalport Youth Hostel*
*Coalport*
*SJ 696 024*
*(1½ miles east off route)*
*tel 0345 371 9325*
*email: coalport@yha.org.uk*

**Stage 9 Ironbridge to Wellington**
The Huntsman Inn
Little Wenlock
tel 01952 503300
http://thehuntsmanoflittlewenlock.co.uk

Buckatree Hall Hotel
The Wrekin
tel 01952 641821
www.buckatreehallhotel.com

Birtley Guest House
Wellington
tel 01952 240483
www.birtley-house-guest-house-telford.
co.uk

Clairmont Guest House
54 Haygate Road
Wellington
tel 01952 414214
http://clairmontguesthouse.co.uk

Lord Nelson
Park Street
Wellington
tel 01952 240055
www.hotelintelford.com

*White House Hotel*
*Watling Street*
*Wellington*
*(¾ mile east off route)*
*tel 01952 250700*
www.telfordwhitehouse.co.uk

Travelodge Telford
Shawbirch (Wellington)
tel 08719 846110
www.travelodge.co.uk

**Stage 10 Wellington to Haughmond**
The Haughmond
Upton Magna
tel 01743 709918
www.thehaughmond.co.uk

The Corbet Arms
Uffington
tel 01743 709232
www.thecorbetarms.com

Travelodge Battlefield
Shrewsbury
tel 0871 984 6120
www.travelodge.co.uk

Ebury Hill Camping & Caravanning
Club site
North of Haughmond Abbey
SJ 546 163
tel 01743 709661
(minimum 2 nights at peak times)

## Stage 11 Haughmond to Wem
Sorrell House
High Street
Grinshill
tel 07706 047230
www.sorrelhousegrinshill.co.uk

The Old Rectory
Wem
tel 01939 233233
www.oldrectorywem.co.uk

*Lower Lacon Caravan Park (camping)*
*SJ 527 295*
*(1 mile east of Wem)*
*tel 01939 232376*
www.llcp.co.uk

## Stage 12 Wem to Ellesmere
*The Moorhead B&B*
*Edstaston*
*SJ 524 318*
*(1 mile east off route)*
*tel 01939 809247*
www.themoorhead.co.uk

Abbey Green Farm (camping and B&B)
Whixall
SJ 506 332
tel 01948 880213
www.abbeygreenfarm.co.uk

Colemere Caravan Park (camping and
glamping)
SJ 431 327
tel 07947 827585
www.colemerecaravanpark.co.uk

Red Lion Coaching Inn
Church Street
Ellesmere
tel 01691 622632
www.redlion-ellesmere.co.uk

## Stage 12A Whitchurch Leg
Bramblewood Caravan Park and Brown
Moss Camping
tel 01948 665399
www.bramblewoodcaravanpark.co.uk

Dodington Lodge (hotel)
tel 01948 662539
www.dodingtonlodge.co.uk

Reubens B&B
7 Pepper Street
Whitchurch
tel 01948 258030
www.reubensbarandbbq.com

Canalside Caravan Park (camping)
Grindley Brook
SJ 523 427
tel 01948 663284
www.canalsidecaravansite.20m.com

## Stage 13 Ellesmere to Llanymynech
Canal Central (camping and café)
Maesbury Marsh
tel 01691 652168
www.canalcentral.uk

The Cross Keys
Llanymynech
tel 01691 831585

## Stage 14 Llanymynech to Nesscliffe
The Bradford Arms
North Road
Llanymynech
tel 01691 830582
www.bradfordarmshotel.co.uk

The Big Bear Lodge (camping and B&B)
Hendre Villa
Melverley Green
tel 01691 682640
www.bigbearlodge.co.uk

Church House Campsite
Melverley
tel 01691 682754
www.churchhousemelverley.co.uk

The Royal Hill (campsite and pub)
Near Edgerley
SJ 351 174
tel 017968 656724

The Old Three Pigeons (pub with room-only accommodation)
Nesscliffe
tel 01743 741279
www.3pigeons.co.uk

**Stage 15 Nesscliffe to Shrewsbury**
Bank House Farm CL
Shrawardine
SJ 400 155
tel 01743 850216
(Caravan & Motorhome Club members only)

Wingfield Park
Montford Bridge Camping
tel 07853 934379
www.thewingfieldcaravanpark.co.uk

Severn House Campsite
Montford Bridge
tel 01743 850229
www.severnhousecampsite.co.uk

Bicton House Camping & Caravanning
Bicton
tel 01743 850054
http://bictoncountryhousepursuits.co.uk

*The Isle B&B*
*Isle Lane*
*Bicton*
*SJ 459 167*
*(1 mile north off route)*
*tel 07776 257286*
www.the-isle-estate.co.uk

**Stretton Skyline Walk**
The Buck's Head
Church Stretton
tel 01694 722898
www.the-bucks-head.co.uk

The Long Mynd Hotel
Church Stretton
tel 0345 4708558
www.hfholidays.co.uk

Mynd House
Little Stretton
tel 01694 722212
www.myndhouse.co.uk

Bridges Long Mynd Youth Hostel
Ratlinghope
SO 395 965
tel 01588 650656
email bridges@yha.org.uk

Womerton Farm Bunkhouse
Near All Stretton
SO 456 973
tel 01694 751260
www.womerton-farm.co.uk

YHA All Stretton (bunkhouse)
SO 455 955
www.yha.org.uk

Small Batch Farm Campsite
Little Stretton
SO 441 920
tel 01694 723358
www.smallbatch-camping.co.uk

# APPENDIX C
*Travel information*

For a buses and trains journey planner, see www.travelinemidlands.co.uk.

**Buses**

**Websites**
* Towns which also have a railway station with links to Shrewsbury

National Express Coaches
www.nationalexpress.com

Arriva Midlands
www.arrivabus.co.uk/midlands

Minsterley Motors
www.minsterleymotors.co.uk

Tanat Valley Coaches
www.tanat.co.uk

Lakeside of Ellesmere
https://lakesidecoaches.co.uk

Please use the following as a guide but check with the previously mentioned websites for up-to-date information.

| Stage | Location | Bus service (to and from Shrewsbury unless stated) | Times (not Sundays or bank holidays unless stated) |
|---|---|---|---|
| 1 | Bayston Hill | Arriva 27 | Every 20min |
| 2 | Bridges | Seasonal shuttle bus | Circular via Minsterley Stiperstones (the Bog) and Church Stretton |
|   | Lydham | Minsterley Motors 553 | 5 per day |
| 3 | Bishop's Castle | Minsterley Motors 553 | 5 per day |
| 4 | Clun | None | |
| 5 | Craven Arms | Minsterley Motors 435 | Hourly via Bromfield |
| 5 | Decoy Cottage A4113SO 457 763 | Arriva 738/740 to/from Ludlow | 4 per day |
| 6 | Ludlow* | Minsterley Motors 435 | Hourly via Bromfield |
| 6 | Clee Hill | R & B Travel 292 to/from Ludlow | Every 2hr |
| 7 | Wheathill | None | |
| 8 | Wilderhope | None | |
|   | Much Wenlock | Arriva 436 | Hourly |
| 9 | Ironbridge | 8, 18, 19 to/from Telford 19 to/from Shrewsbury | Hourly |

| Stage | Location | Bus service (to and from Shrewsbury unless stated) | Times (not Sundays or bank holidays unless stated) |
|---|---|---|---|
| 10 | Wellington* | | |
| | Admaston and Rodington | Arriva 16 to/from Wellington | |
| 11 | Haughmond Abbey | Arriva 519 | Every 2hr |
| 11 | Hadnall | Arriva 511 to Shrewsbury & Whitchurch | Hourly |
| 11 | Quarry View, Clive | Arriva 511 to Shrewsbury & Whitchurch | Hourly |
| 12 | Wem | Arriva 511 to Shrewsbury & Whitchurch | Hourly |
| 12A | Whitchurch* | Arriva 512 to Shrewsbury & Whitchurch | Hourly |
| 12A | Prees Heath | Arriva 513 to Shrewsbury & Whitchurch | Hourly |
| 13 | Ellesmere | Lakeside 501 | 5 per day (school days only) |
| 13 | Maesbury Marsh | Arriva 576 | Every 2hr |
| 13 | Queen's Head | Arriva 70a | Every 30min |
| 14 | Llanymynech | 72 to Oswestry | 7 times a day |
| 15 | Nesscliffe | Arriva 70/70a | Every 30min |
| 15 | Bicton | Arriva 70/70a | Every 30min |
| 15 | Montford Bridge Shelton | Arriva 70/70a | Every 30min |

* Towns which also have a railway station with links to Shrewsbury

## Railways

### Websites
Transport for Wales
https://tfwrail.wales

London Midland Trains
www.londonnorthwesternrailway.co.uk

Heart of Wales Line (Swansea)
www.heart-of-wales.co.uk

Virgin Trains
www.virgintrains.co.uk

### Getting there
Manchester to Shrewsbury via Whitchurch with some services to Wem

Birmingham to Shrewsbury to (connections to London, East Midlands and North)

Milford Haven/Carmarthen/Cardiff/
Swansea to Shrewsbury

Swansea to Shrewsbury via Builth Wells
and Craven Arms

Holyhead and Chester to Shrewsbury

**Getting around**
Ludlow to Shrewsbury (via Church
Stretton, Craven Arms and Ludlow)

Wellington to Shrewsbury

Shrewsbury to Whitchurch (via Wem,
Yorton (for Grinshill) and Prees)

*Taxi companies (selected)*
AAA, Shrewsbury
tel 01743 244555

Bishop's Castle Taxis
tel 07551 825931

Rez's Cab, Craven Arms
tel 07487 899102

Ludlow Taxis
tel 01584 876666

Teaky's Taxis, Ludlow
tel 01584 879478

Go Carz, Telford
tel 01952 501050

Wem Taxis, Wem
tel 07904 669149

Dell's Taxis, Whitchurch
tel 07761 083174

Oswestry Cabs
tel 01691 661663

# APPENDIX D
*Useful contacts*

**Tourist Information Centres**

**Shrewsbury**
Museum and Art Gallery
The Square
tel 01743 258888
email: visitorinfo@shropshire.gov.uk

**Craven Arms**
Shropshire Hills Discovery Centre
School Road
tel 01588 676060
email: info@shropshirehillsdiscovery
centre.co.uk

**Ludlow**
Ludlow Assembly Rooms
Mill Street
tel 01584 875053
email: visitors@ludlowassembly
rooms.co.uk

**Much Wenlock**
The Museum
High Street
tel 01952 727679
email: muchwenlock.tourism@
shropshire.gov.uk

**Ironbridge**
Coach Road
Coalbrookdale
tel 01952 433424
email: tic@ironbridge.org.uk

**Whitchurch**
Civic Centre
High Street
tel 01948 665761
email: info@whitchurchcouncil.uk

**Other useful websites**
Shropshire Way Association
Your first port of call for the latest
news on the Shropshire Way,
accommodation, transport, contact
details should be:
https://shropshireway.org.uk

Shropshire's Great Outdoors
Information about activities in
Shropshire
www.shropshiresgreatoutdoors.co.uk

Shropshire Council
tel 0345 6789000
www.shropshire.gov.uk

Telford and Wrekin Council
tel 01952 380000
www.telford.gov.uk

Shropshire Hills Area of Outstanding
National Beauty (AONB)
www.shropshirehillsaonb.co.uk

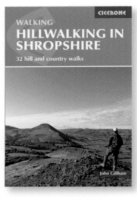

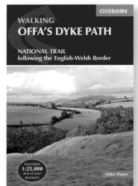
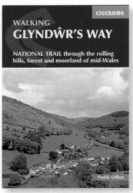

# LISTING OF CICERONE GUIDES

## SCOTLAND

Backpacker's Britain:
   Northern Scotland
Ben Nevis and Glen Coe
Cycle Touring in Northern Scotland
Cycling in the Hebrides
Great Mountain Days in Scotland
Mountain Biking in Southern and
   Central Scotland
Mountain Biking in West and North
   West Scotland
Not the West Highland Way
Scotland
Scotland's Best Small Mountains
Scotland's Mountain Ridges
The Ayrshire and Arran Coastal Paths
The Border Country
The Borders Abbeys Way
The Cape Wrath Trail
The Great Glen Way
The Great Glen Way Map Booklet
The Hebridean Way
The Hebrides
The Isle of Mull
The Isle of Skye
The Skye Trail
The Southern Upland Way
The Speyside Way
The Speyside Way Map Booklet
The West Highland Way
Walking Highland Perthshire
Walking in Scotland's Far North
Walking in the Angus Glens
Walking in the Cairngorms
Walking in the Ochils, Campsie Fells
   and Lomond Hills
Walking in the Pentland Hills
Walking in the Southern Uplands
Walking in Torridon
Walking Loch Lomond and the
   Trossachs
Walking on Arran
Walking on Harris and Lewis
Walking on Jura, Islay and Colonsay
Walking on Rum and the Small Isles
Walking on the Orkney and
   Shetland Isles
Walking on Uist and Barra
Walking the Corbetts
   Vol 1 South of the Great Glen
Walking the Corbetts
   Vol 2 North of the Great Glen
Walking the Galloway Hills
Walking the Munros Vol 1 – Southern,
   Central and Western Highlands
Walking the Munros Vol 2 – Northern
   Highlands and the Cairngorms
West Highland Way Map Booklet
Winter Climbs Ben Nevis and
   Glen Coe
Winter Climbs in the Cairngorms

## NORTHERN ENGLAND TRAILS

Hadrian's Wall Path
Hadrian's Wall Path Map Booklet
Pennine Way Map Booklet
The Coast to Coast Map Booklet
The Coast to Coast Walk
The Dales Way
The Dales Way Map Booklet
The Pennine Way

## LAKE DISTRICT

Cycling in the Lake District
Great Mountain Days in the
   Lake District
Lake District Winter Climbs
Lake District:
   High Level and Fell Walks
Lake District:
   Low Level and Lake Walks
Mountain Biking in the Lake District
Outdoor Adventures with Children –
   Lake District
Scafell Pike
Scrambles in the Lake District – North
Scrambles in the Lake District – South
Short Walks in Lakeland Book 2:
   North Lakeland
The Cumbria Way
The Southern Fells
Tour of the Lake District
Trail and Fell Running in the
   Lake District
Walking the Lake District Fells –
   Langdale
Walking the Lake District Fells –
   Wasdale

## NORTH WEST ENGLAND AND
## THE ISLE OF MAN

Cycling the Pennine Bridleway
Cycling the Way of the Roses
Isle of Man Coastal Path
The Lancashire Cycleway
The Lune Valley and Howgills
The Ribble Way
Walking in Cumbria's Eden Valley
Walking in Lancashire
Walking in the Forest of Bowland
   and Pendle
Walking on the Isle of Man
Walking on the West Pennine Moors
Walks in Ribble Country
Walks in Silverdale and Arnside

## NORTH EAST ENGLAND,
## YORKSHIRE DALES AND
## PENNINES

Cycling in the Yorkshire Dales
Great Mountain Days in the Pennines
Mountain Biking in the
   Yorkshire Dales

South Pennine Walks
St Oswald's Way and St Cuthbert's
   Way
The Cleveland Way and the Yorkshire
   Wolds Way
The Cleveland Way Map Booklet
The North York Moors
The Reivers Way
The Teesdale Way
Trail and Fell Running in the
   Yorkshire Dales
Walking in County Durham
Walking in Northumberland
Walking in the North Pennines
Walking in the Yorkshire Dales:
   North and East
Walking in the Yorkshire Dales:
   South and West
Walks in the Yorkshire Dales

## WALES AND WELSH BORDERS

Cycle Touring in Wales
Cycling Lon Las Cymru
Glyndwr's Way
Great Mountain Days in Snowdonia
Hillwalking in Shropshire
Hillwalking in Wales – Vol 1
Hillwalking in Wales – Vol 2
Mountain Walking in Snowdonia
Offa's Dyke Map Booklet
Offa's Dyke Path
Pembrokeshire Coast Path
   Map Booklet
Ridges of Snowdonia
Scrambles in Snowdonia
Snowdonia: Low-level and easy
   walks – North
The Cambrian Way
The Ceredigion and Snowdonia
   Coast Paths
The Pembrokeshire Coast Path
The Severn Way
The Snowdonia Way
The Wales Coast Path
The Wye Valley Walk
Walking in Carmarthenshire
Walking in Pembrokeshire
Walking in the Forest of Dean
Walking in the Wye Valley
Walking on the Brecon Beacons
Walking on the Gower
Walking the Shropshire Way

## DERBYSHIRE, PEAK DISTRICT
## AND MIDLANDS

Cycling in the Peak District
Dark Peak Walks
Scrambles in the Dark Peak
Walking in Derbyshire

White Peak Walks:
   The Northern Dales
White Peak Walks:
   The Southern Dales

## SOUTHERN ENGLAND

20 Classic Sportive Rides in
   South East England
20 Classic Sportive Rides in
   South West England
Cycling in the Cotswolds
Mountain Biking on the North Downs
Mountain Biking on the South Downs
North Downs Way Map Booklet
South West Coast Path Map Booklet –
   Vol 1: Minehead to St Ives
South West Coast Path Map Booklet –
   Vol 2: St Ives to Plymouth
South West Coast Path Map Booklet –
   Vol 3: Plymouth to Poole
Suffolk Coast and Heath Walks
The Cotswold Way
The Cotswold Way Map Booklet
The Great Stones Way
The Kennet and Avon Canal
The Lea Valley Walk
The North Downs Way
The Peddars Way and Norfolk
   Coast path
The Pilgrims' Way
The Ridgeway Map Booklet
The Ridgeway National Trail
The South Downs Way
The South Downs Way Map Booklet
The South West Coast Path
The Thames Path
The Thames Path Map Booklet
The Two Moors Way
Two Moors Way Map Booklet
Walking Hampshire's Test Way
Walking in Cornwall
Walking in Essex
Walking in Kent
Walking in London
Walking in Norfolk
Walking in Sussex
Walking in the Chilterns
Walking in the Cotswolds
Walking in the Isles of Scilly
Walking in the New Forest
Walking in the North Wessex Downs
Walking in the Thames Valley
Walking on Dartmoor
Walking on Guernsey
Walking on Jersey
Walking on the Isle of Wight
Walking the Jurassic Coast
Walks in the South Downs
   National Park

## BRITISH ISLES CHALLENGES, COLLECTIONS AND ACTIVITIES

The Big Rounds
The Book of the Bivvy
The Book of the Bothy
The C2C Cycle Route
The End to End Cycle Route
The End to End Trail
The Mountains of England and Wales:
   Vol 1 Wales
The Mountains of England and Wales:
   Vol 2 England
The National Trails
The UK's County Tops
Three Peaks, Ten Tors

## ALPS CROSS-BORDER ROUTES

100 Hut Walks in the Alps
Across the Eastern Alps: E5
Alpine Ski Mountaineering
   Vol 1 – Western Alps
Alpine Ski Mountaineering
   Vol 2 – Central and Eastern Alps
Chamonix to Zermatt
The Karnischer Hohenweg
The Tour of the Bernina
Tour of Mont Blanc
Tour of Monte Rosa
Tour of the Matterhorn
Trail Running – Chamonix and the
   Mont Blanc region
Trekking in the Alps
Trekking in the Silvretta and
   Ratikon Alps
Trekking Munich to Venice
Walking in the Alps

## PYRENEES AND FRANCE/SPAIN CROSS-BORDER ROUTES

Shorter Treks in the Pyrenees
The GR10 Trail
The GR11 Trail
The Pyrenean Haute Route
The Pyrenees
Walks and Climbs in the Pyrenees

## AUSTRIA

Innsbruck Mountain Adventures
The Adlerweg
Trekking in Austria's Hohe Tauern
Trekking in the Stubai Alps
Trekking in the Zillertal Alps
Walking in Austria

## SWITZERLAND

Switzerland's Jura Crest Trail
The Swiss Alpine Pass Route –
   Via Alpina Route 1
The Swiss Alps
Tour of the Jungfrau Region
Walking in the Bernese Oberland
Walking in the Engadine – Switzerland
Walking in the Valais

## FRANCE

Chamonix Mountain Adventures
Cycle Touring in France
Cycling London to Paris
Cycling the Canal de la Garonne
Cycling the Canal du Midi
Écrins National Park
Mont Blanc Walks
Mountain Adventures in
   the Maurienne
The GR20 Corsica
The GR5 Trail
The GR5 Trail – Vosges and Jura
The Grand Traverse of the
   Massif Central
The Loire Cycle Route
The Moselle Cycle Route
The River Rhone Cycle Route
The Robert Louis Stevenson Trail
The Way of St James – Le Puy to the
   Pyrenees
Tour of the Oisans: The GR54
Tour of the Queyras
Vanoise Ski Touring
Via Ferratas of the French Alps
Walking in Corsica
Walking in Provence – East
Walking in Provence – West
Walking in the Auvergne
Walking in the Briannonais
Walking in the Cevennes
Walking in the Dordogne
Walking in the Haute Savoie: North
Walking in the Haute Savoie: South
Walks in the Cathar Region

## GERMANY

Hiking and Cycling in the Black Forest
The Danube Cycleway Vol 1
The Rhine Cycle Route
The Westweg
Walking in the Bavarian Alps

## ICELAND AND GREENLAND

Trekking in Greenland – The Arctic
   Circle Trail
Walking and Trekking in Iceland

## IRELAND

The Wild Atlantic Way and
   Western Ireland

## ITALY

Italy's Sibillini National Park
Shorter Walks in the Dolomites
Ski Touring and Snowshoeing in
   the Dolomites
The Way of St Francis
Through the Italian Alps
Trekking in the Apennines
Trekking in the Dolomites
Via Ferratas of the
   Italian Dolomites Vol 1
Via Ferratas of the
   Italian Dolomites: Vol 2
Walking and Trekking in the
   Gran Paradiso

Walking in Abruzzo
Walking in Italy's Cinque Terre
Walking in Italy's Stelvio
  National Park
Walking in Sardinia
Walking in Sicily
Walking in the Dolomites
Walking in Tuscany
Walking in Umbria
Walking Lake Como and Maggiore
Walking Lake Garda and Iseo
Walking on the Amalfi Coast
Walks and Treks in the Maritime Alps

**BELGIUM AND LUXEMBOURG**
The GR5 Trail – Benelux and Lorraine
Walking in the Ardennes

**SCANDINAVIA:
NORWAY, SWEDEN, FINLAND**
Trekking the Kungsleden
Walking in Norway

**POLAND, SLOVAKIA,
ROMANIA, HUNGARY
AND BULGARIA**
The Danube Cycleway Volume 2
The High Tatras
The Mountains of Romania
Walking in Bulgaria's National Parks
Walking in Hungary

**SLOVENIA, CROATIA, SERBIA,
MONTENEGRO, ALBANIA
AND KOSOVO**
Mountain Biking in Slovenia
The Islands of Croatia
The Julian Alps of Slovenia
The Mountains of Montenegro
The Peaks of the Balkans Trail
The Slovene Mountain Trail
Walking in Slovenia: The Karavanke
Walks and Treks in Croatia

**SPAIN**
Camino de Santiago – Camino Frances
Coastal Walks in Andalucia
Cycle Touring in Spain
Cycling the Camino de Santiago
Mountain Walking in Mallorca
Mountain Walking in
  Southern Catalunya
Spain's Sendero Historico: The GR1
The Andalucian Coast to Coast Walk
The Camino del Norte and
  Camino Primitivo
The Camino Ingles and Ruta do Mar
The Mountains of Nerja
The Mountains of Ronda
  and Grazalema
The Northern Caminos
The Sierras of Extremadura
Trekking in Mallorca

Trekking in the Canary Islands
Walking and Trekking in the
  Sierra Nevada
Walking in Andalucia
Walking in Menorca
Walking in the Cordillera Cantabrica
Walking on Gran Canaria
Walking on La Gomera and El Hierro
Walking on La Palma
Walking on Lanzarote and
  Fuerteventura
Walking on Tenerife
Walking on the Costa Blanca
Walking the Camino dos Faros

**PORTUGAL**
Portugal's Rota Vicentina
The Camino Portugues
Walking in Portugal
Walking in the Algarve
Walking on Madeira
Walking on the Azores

**GREECE**
The High Mountains of Crete
Trekking in Greece
Walking and Trekking in Zagori
Walking and Trekking on Corfu

**CYPRUS**
Walking in Cyprus

**MALTA**
Walking on Malta

**INTERNATIONAL CHALLENGES,
COLLECTIONS AND ACTIVITIES**
Canyoning in the Alps
Europe's High Points
The Via Francigena Canterbury to
  Rome – Part 2

**MOROCCO**
Mountaineering in the Moroccan
  High Atlas
The High Atlas
Walks and Scrambles in the Moroccan
  Anti-Atlas

**TANZANIA**
Kilimanjaro

**SOUTH AFRICA**
Walking in the Drakensberg

**TAJIKISTAN**
Trekking in Tajikistan

**JAPAN**
Hiking and Trekking in the Japan Alps
  and Mount Fuji
Japan's Kumano Kodo Pilgrimage

**JORDAN**
Jordan – Walks, Treks, Caves, Climbs
  and Canyons
Treks and Climbs in Wadi Rum,
  Jordan

**NEPAL**
Annapurna
Everest: A Trekker's Guide
Trekking in the Himalaya

**BHUTAN**
Trekking in Bhutan

**INDIA**
Trekking in Ladakh

**CHINA**
The Mount Kailash Trek

**NORTH AMERICA:
USA AND CANADA**
The John Muir Trail
The Pacific Crest Trail

**SOUTH AMERICA:
ARGENTINA, CHILE AND PERU**
Aconcagua and the Southern Andes
Hiking and Biking Peru's Inca Trails
Torres del Paine

**TECHNIQUES**
Fastpacking
Geocaching in the UK
Lightweight Camping
Map and Compass
Outdoor Photography
Polar Exploration
Rock Climbing
Sport Climbing
The Mountain Hut Book

**MINI GUIDES**
Alpine Flowers
Avalanche!
Navigation
Pocket First Aid and Wilderness
  Medicine
Snow

**MOUNTAIN LITERATURE**
8000 metres
A Walk in the Clouds
Abode of the Gods
Fifty Years of Adventure
The Pennine Way – the Path,
  the People, the Journey
Unjustifiable Risk?

For full information on all our guides,
books and eBooks, visit our website:
**www.cicerone.co.uk**

# Explore the world with Cicerone

walking • trekking • mountaineering • climbing • mountain biking •
cycling • via ferratas • scrambling • trail running • skills and techniques

For over 50 years, Cicerone have built up an outstanding collection of
nearly 400 guides, inspiring all sorts of amazing experiences.

## www.cicerone.co.uk – where adventures begin

- Our **website** is a treasure-trove for every outdoor adventurer. You
  can buy books or read inspiring articles and trip reports, get technical
  advice, check for updates, and view videos, photographs and mapping
  for routes and treks.

- **Register this book** or any other Cicerone guide in your member's
  library on our website and you can choose to automatically access
  updates and GPX files for your books, if available.

- Our **fortnightly newsletters** will update you on new publications and
  articles and keep you informed of other news and events. You can also
  follow us on Facebook, Twitter and Instagram.

We hope you have enjoyed using this guidebook. If you have any
comments you would like to share, please contact us using the form on
our website or via email, so that we can provide the best experience for
future customers.

## CICERONE

Juniper House, Murley Moss Business Village, Oxenholme Road, Kendal LA9 7RL

 info@cicerone.co.uk              cicerone.co.uk